Comments on other *Amazing Stories* from readers & reviewers

"Tightly written volumes filled with lots of wit and humour about famous and infamous Canadians."
Eric Shackleton, *The Globe and Mail*

"The heightened sense of drama and intrigue, combined with a good dose of human interest is what sets Amazing Stories *apart."*
Pamela Klaffke, *Calgary Herald*

"This is popular history as it should be... For this price, buy two and give one to a friend."
Terry Cook, a reader from Ottawa, on **Rebel Women**

"Glasner creates the moment of the explosion itself in graphic detail...she builds detail upon gruesome detail to create a convincingly authentic picture."
Peggy McKinnon, *The Sunday Herald*, on **The Halifax Explosion**

"It was wonderful...I found I could not put it down. I was sorry when it was completed."
Dorothy F. from Manitoba on **Marie-Anne Lagimodière**

"Stories are rich in description, and bristle with a clever, stylish realness."
Mark Weber, *Central Alberta Advisor*, on **Ghost Town Stories II**

"A compelling read. Bertin...has selected only the most intriguing tales, which she narrates with a wealth of detail."
Joyce Glasner, *New Brunswick Reader*, on **Strange Events**

"The resulting book is one readers will want to share with all the women in their lives."
Lynn Martel, *Rocky Mountain Outlook*, on **Women Explorers**

STRANGE EVENTS
AND MORE

AMAZING STORIES

STRANGE EVENTS AND MORE

Canadian Giants, Witches, Wizards, and Other Tales

MYSTERY/HISTORY

by Johanna Bertin

PUBLISHED BY ALTITUDE PUBLISHING CANADA LTD.
1500 Railway Avenue, Canmore, Alberta T1W 1P6
www.altitudepublishing.com
1-800-957-6888

Extreme care has been taken to ensure that all information presented in
this book is accurate and up to date. Neither the author nor the
publisher can be held responsible for any errors.

Publisher	Stephen Hutchings
Associate Publisher	Kara Turner
Series Editor	Jill Foran
Editor	Nancy Mackenzie
Digital photo colouring & map	Bryan Pezzi

We acknowledge the financial support of the Government
of Canada through the Book Publishing Industry Development
Program (BPIDP) for our publishing activities.

Altitude GreenTree Program
Altitude Publishing will plant twice as many trees as were used
in the manufacturing of this product.

We acknowledge the support of the Canada Council for the Arts which
in 2003 invested $21.7 million in writing and publishing throughout Canada.

Canada Council   Conseil des Arts
for the Arts   du Canada

National Library of Canada Cataloguing in Publication Data

Bertin, Johanna
Strange events and more / Johanna Bertin.

(Amazing stories)
ISBN 1-55153-783-4

1. Curiosities and wonders--Canada. I. Title. II. Series: Amazing stories (Canmore, Alta.)
AG243.B474 2004   001.94'0971   C2004-902705-0

Printed and bound in Canada by Friesens
2 4 6 8 9 7 5 3 1

To my children Geoff and Catharine,
with much love.

Contents

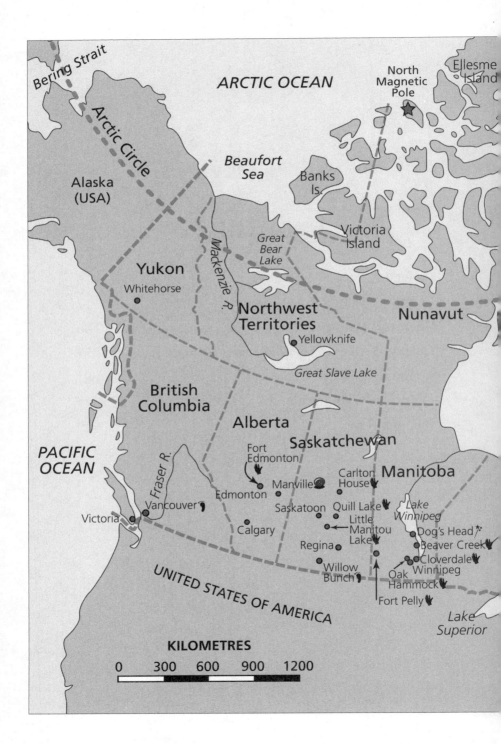

Bering Strait

Arctic Circle

ARCTIC OCEAN

North Magnetic Pole

Ellesme Island

Beaufort Sea

Banks Is.

Alaska (USA)

Victoria Island

Great Bear Lake

Mackenzie R.

Yukon

Whitehorse

Northwest Territories

Nunavut

Yellowknife

Great Slave Lake

British Columbia

Alberta

Saskatchewan

Manitoba

PACIFIC OCEAN

Fraser R.

Fort Edmonton

Carlton House

Manville

Edmonton

Saskatoon

Quill Lake

Lake Winnipeg

Vancouver

Little Manitou Lake

Victoria

Calgary

Dog's Head

Beaver Creek

Regina

Cloverdale

Winnipeg

UNITED STATES OF AMERICA

Willow Bunch

Oak Hammock

Fort Pelly

Lake Superior

KILOMETRES

0   300   600   900   1200

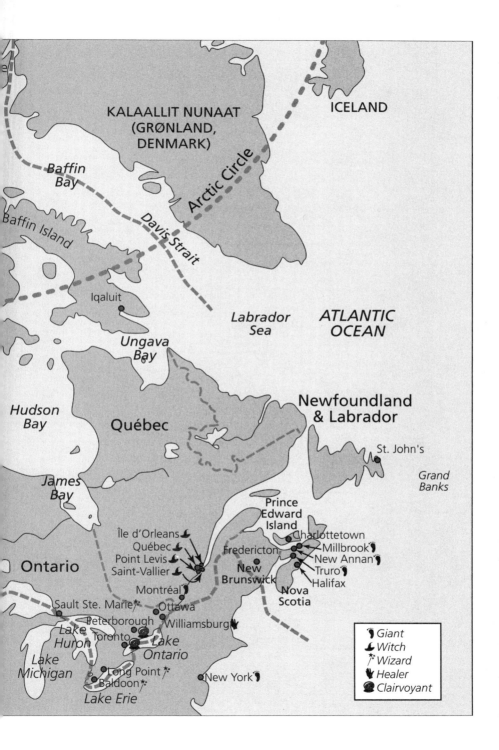

KALAALLIT NUNAAT
(GRØNLAND,
DENMARK)

ICELAND

Baffin
Bay

Arctic Circle

Davis Strait

Baffin Island

Iqaluit

Labrador
Sea

ATLANTIC
OCEAN

Ungava
Bay

Hudson
Bay

Québec

Newfoundland
& Labrador

St. John's

James
Bay

Grand
Banks

Prince
Edward
Island

Charlottetown

Île d'Orleans

Québec

Point Levis

Saint-Vallier

Fredericton

Millbrook

New Annan

Truro

Halifax

New
Brunswick

Ontario

Montréal

Nova
Scotia

Sault Ste. Marie

Ottawa

Peterborough

Williamsburg

Lake
Huron

Toronto

Lake
Ontario

Lake
Michigan

Long Point

Baldoon

New York

Lake Erie

🧍	Giant
↙	Witch
🦶	Wizard
✋	Healer
🐚	Clairvoyant

Prologue

The Vancouver Police were worried. They held a suspect in a jewel robbery that had occurred two weeks ago, but had no evidence that would allow them to keep him in custody. Time was running out. If they couldn't recover the jewels soon, they would have to let the man go. Once he was free, they knew he would dispose of the jewels.

The police consulted Dr. Otto Maximilian Langsner, a mind reader who had done covert work for the British government. They told him about the jewel heist and their suspect. The problem was that they had no proof and no jewels. Would Dr. Langsner be willing to "read" the suspect's mind and tell them what he was able to find out? Dr. Langsner agreed, and was escorted to the interview room where the police had placed the man.

Dr. Langsner quietly entered the room and sat in a chair. He said nothing to the suspect and nothing to the guard who sat beside the man. Dr. Langsner just sat and watched the prisoner. The prisoner spoke to Dr. Langsner, but got no response. He swore at him, but by nary a flinch or a twitch of the eye did Dr. Langsner even acknowledge that he had heard the man. The suspect raised his arm as if to hit Dr. Langsner, but the guard warned him off.

After 10 minutes, the suspect began to fidget. After 20, even the guard was getting spooked. Dr. Langsner continued to sit quietly, hardly moving. His eyes never left the suspect.

After 30 minutes, Dr. Langsner turned to the guard, startling him with his sudden movement after being still for so long. He said that he was finished and asked the guard to let the detectives know that he was ready to leave. The guard signalled, and the door to the interview room opened. Dr. Langsner stepped out of the room.

"I can tell you where you will find the jewels," he said.

Chapter 1
Giants

yths and legends abound with tales of giants — people of huge strength and fierce disposition. Canada's giants are remembered for their gentleness and for the dignity with which they met the challenges created by their size. Two giants — Anna Swan Bates and Edouard Beaupre — succeeded in creating active, fulfilled lives. Only one of them, however, would be allowed a death with dignity.

Anna Swan Bates: Friend to Kings and Queens
On August 6, 1846, a log house in the small village of Millbrook, Nova Scotia, was abuzz with visitors. They had come to see Anna, the Swans' beautiful and healthy newborn baby girl. What brought the visitors was her size — she was

an unbelievable 18 pounds. Coming into the world the size of a six-month-old was but the first of many challenges Anna would face throughout her life.

Anna's parents were not wealthy people, but Scottish immigrants who were seeking a chance to farm their own land, not that of rich landlords. They had three children now, and were to have nine more after Anna. The expense of custom-made shoes for their giant daughter was not something they could afford.

So in March 1851, when Anna was four years old, her father took her to the Halifax Exhibition, where she appeared as the "Infant Giantess." She was already four feet tall. A local newspaper did a feature about her in which she was described as "rosy as a milkmaid, weighed over 94 pounds, and already had arms and wrists as large as a full-grown man." As Anna gained fame for her gigantism, she was able to contribute to the financial security of her family. Her appearances at the exhibition paid for new shoes for the entire family, including custom-made shoes for her from the cobbler in New Glasgow.

While Anna helped with the costs of her huge family, she was not taken advantage of. Her parents, and indeed the whole community, were fiercely proud and protective of her right to be an individual. By age seven, she was often mistaken for an adult, an intellectually delayed adult. One cattle buyer made the mistake of calling Anna a "daftee." No one sold him cattle. A visiting Presbyterian minister said that he had met Anna and her mother in a buggy. "I could not help but stare at this monstrosity and wonder what she had had for breakfast," he told his friends.

Anna's parents and neighbours were above all this. "Annie, stand tall lass, and be proud of your Highland ancestry," they told her. And that is how Anna led her life. She never stooped or slumped her shoulders. Instead, she adapted to her surroundings.

Anna could not sit comfortably at the kitchen table, so she sat on the floor at meals and still managed to have her head at the same level as her siblings. Her family modified the house as best they could, taking down a dividing wall between her bedroom and the next and building her a special, large bed. Her clothing was a major expense requiring yards and yards of material.

Phineas T. Barnum, founder of the Barnum & Bailey Circus, had heard rumours of Anna over the years. The story of the baby's huge birth weight had made it all the way to Boston on the cargo ships that plied the waters between Nova Scotia and the Eastern Seaboard. Barnum sent a scout to Nova Scotia to learn whether she really was the giant that she was rumoured to be. When the scout's report was better than he had imagined, Barnum sent Anna an offer to join his show of the unusual. Anna turned it down. She had always loved children, was a good student, and wanted to become a teacher. As a young girl, she had sat on the hill behind the house and played school, teaching the village children how to read. At 15, her parents also felt that she was too young to go off, unsupervised, to New York. Such a large city would have seemed a very dangerous place to people of New Annan, where the Swans now lived.

While Anna had not felt ready for New York, she knew that she would have to leave home to attend the Normal School in Truro if she were to obtain her teacher's certificate. So, at age 15 she moved in with an aunt who lived in Truro. Life there was not easy for Anna. Her huge size made her a curiosity and people stared at her in frank amazement. People sniggered. They gawked at her. They followed her and taunted her. Unable to feel at ease in Truro, Anna returned to New Annan, where everybody accepted her as the Swans' big girl.

Anna continued to grow taller. By the age of 17, she measured 7 feet, 11½ inches and weighed close to 400 pounds. She was no longer the sheltered young woman she had been before her painful experience in Truro. Anna made a decision. If she couldn't be a teacher, she would have to find another way to be self-supporting. She was sure that there would be a lot of children attending the Barnum show. Perhaps she could find a way to combine her love of teaching and her love of children with her new job. She told Barnum that she was ready to consider his offer of a job. On hearing this, Barnum arranged passage for Anna and her parents to travel to New York to discuss the offer and see what kind of a life Anna would have.

Giants

Anna Swan with her parents

Barnum's American Museum was unlike anything Anna or her parents had seen before. Located in a five-storey building on Broadway in the heart of downtown New York, the building was full of curiosities. There were works of taxidermy and live displays of exotic animals. There were displays of minerals and fossils. There were jugglers, ventriloquists, and trick dogs. And there were unusual people like Anna — giants, albinos, dwarves, and Siamese twins. As much as possible, it was a tasteful exhibit with the ticket holders touring the various venues in the different areas. Anna would not simply be on display. She was well read and loved music. Anna would perform plays, give lectures on gigantism, and play the piano. Most importantly for Anna, Barnum promised that she would have a tutor, music lessons, and steady employment.

At $23 per week to be paid in gold, Anna would be self-supporting. She accepted Barnum's offer. Sometimes she worked alone, playing the piano for her audience. Other times Commodore Nott, a dwarf measuring only 29 inches tall, accompanied her. People paid five cents to see Anna or listen to her lectures. For an extra five cents, they could purchase a postcard with her picture.

Anna now had access to more books than she could read in a lifetime. When Barnum told Anna that he planned to take her to Europe, she realized that she was going to have an opportunity to visit those places that she had read about. She wanted to see Dumfries, her ancestral home. Barnum told her that he would take her there, but first she was to be presented to Queen Victoria.

In 1863, Barnum took his American Museum to England. Anna was presented to Queen Victoria and evidently made quite an impression. After eight months of touring, they returned to America and the comparative quiet existence of her life in her quarters at the museum. It was the location of that apartment that almost cost Anna her life.

On July 13, 1865, the museum caught fire and Anna was

trapped in her apartment on the third floor. It was too risky for her to try and make it down the stairs. Not only was there no time, but the firemen did not feel that the stairs, weakened by the heat and flames, would support her weight. Besides, the route down the stairs would take Anna into the heart of the inferno. Her plight was desperate.

In the burning museum there was an even greater danger than the flames. Many of the animals in the museum were loose in the hallways — either freed by their keepers in the hope that they would manage to get out of the building, or escaped from their cages. While the fire raced up the stairs, a lion and a lioness tried to go down. Two kangaroos had come up from their quarters on the second floor, to be met by a Bengal tiger and a polar bear at the landing. Monkeys and an orangutan had escaped via the windows and had climbed onto neighbouring buildings. Parrots, mockingbirds, vultures, eagles, and condors flew in confusion. All around Anna were the terrible screams of people and animals trapped and on fire.

"It seemed absolutely hopeless," reported the *New York Times*. But the museum employees were an inventive group, and with the help of the New York Fire Department they "procured a lofty derrick [crane] ... and erected it alongside the museum. A portion of the wall was broken off on each side of the window, the strong tackle was got in readiness, the tall woman was made fast to one end and swung over the heads of the people in the street, with eighteen men grasping the other extremity of the line, and lowered down from the third story, amid enthusiastic applause. A carriage of extraordinary capacity was in readiness, and entering this the young lady was driven away to a hotel." A cheer went up from the thousands of people who had gathered. By nightfall, 40,000 had come to see the ruins and the site of the marvellous rescue.

Anna was safe, but she had lost all her savings, her clothing, and her belongings. She returned to Nova Scotia to recover and rest while the museum was relocated to new premises. Her participation in the museum met with disapproval from her local clergyman, who used a sermon to warn women about exhibiting themselves in the circus. "It's one thing for men, another for women," said a clergyman identified only as W.M.P.

Later that year, Anna rejoined Barnum at his new museum. On March 3, 1868, that building burned down, too! It was this second fire that was to inadvertently be the cause of Anna falling in love.

In the hiatus caused by the loss of the second museum, Anna travelled to New Jersey with friends. There, she met Captain Martin Van Buren Bates, a Confederate Army officer known as the "Kentucky Giant." Bates was actually shorter than Anna, measuring only seven feet, nine inches. A close friendship developed, but Anna returned to Barnum's and began a second eight-month tour of Europe. She continued working with him until 1871, when her contract with Barnum was completed. Anna then decided to join Judge H.P. Ingalls on a planned three-year tour of Europe. Fate was to take a turn here. When she arrived at dockside to board the ocean liner, she had no inkling of who one of her travelling companions was to be.

Captain Bates had also booked passage on the *City of Brussels*. On April 22, 1871, the ocean voyage began. Before they disembarked at Liverpool, England, the couple would announce their engagement. Both had had proposals of marriage in the past, proposals they had turned down fearing that their suitors had been motivated by a desire to join in the celebrity and financial rewards of their large mates. But this relationship was different. Anna and Martin truly loved each other.

At Liverpool, news of the engagement brought the press. It was remarked that "Martin and Anna were devoid of the vulgarity so common to show people but were instead graceful, cultured, refined in manners and well-spoken." The couple was soon besieged with invitations — and a royal command. Queen Victoria, who had met both Anna and Martin previously and liked them both, wished them to attend her at Windsor Castle. She insisted that the couple wed at the Royal Parish of St. Martin-in-the-Fields, London. As a special gesture, Queen Victoria offered to have Anna's wedding gown designed and made by the royal dressmakers.

On June 17, 1871, Martin and Anna were wed. Anna was resplendent in the wedding dress and veil given to her by the queen. One hundred yards of satin and fifty yards of lace had gone into the making of the gown. On one of Anna's fingers sat a diamond cluster ring, and both Martin and Anna wore large gold watches — all were gifts from Queen Victoria. The gold chain on Anna's watch was said to measure six feet in length. The wedding guest list was eclectic. Mingling amidst Anna's friends from the Judge H.P. Ingalls Show — who included Tom Thumb the dwarf and the "Two-headed Nightingale," a pair of co-joined or Siamese twins famous for their beautiful duets (one sang soprano and the other contralto) — were the two British physicians that Anna and Martin had consulted when she had agreed to marry him.

Anna wanted a family. But she didn't know whether her condition (a benign brain tumour on the pituitary gland) would prevent her from conceiving a child. She was examined by Dr. James Simpson and others and declared to be "fit with healthy organs, though proportionally enlarged."

Anna, relieved and hopeful, was soon pregnant and shared the news with her family in Nova Scotia. Her health was good, so she and Martin carried on with their activities and performances. As giants, in fact as the only known wedded giants in the world, they were in great demand and spent much of their extended honeymoon as guests of European royalty. They visited the Royal Family of Luxembourg, the King of Belgium, and the Princess of Wales. Anna continued to write home, creating vivid pictures of the people she met and the palaces she stayed in. Her most exciting news was contained in the updates she gave her family on her pregnancy. As the time for Anna to give birth drew near, the Bates returned to England to deliver their child. They wanted Doctors Cross and Buckland to deliver the baby.

On March 19, 1872, Anna delivered a beautiful, but still-born, baby girl. Like Anna at birth, the infant girl weighed 18 pounds and measured 27 inches in length. Grief-stricken, the couple donated their baby to the London Hospital, hoping that she might be able to provide some clue as to the reason for their and her gigantism.

Anna and Martin were distraught. They had taken every precaution to ensure a healthy baby. They wrote letters home, not excited letters filled with the joyous news of their baby's birth, but painful letters filled with despair and self-blame. They hoped for some explanation of their baby's death. They hoped for some directions about how to keep another baby safe, but there was nothing.

For two more years, the Bates remained in England, but they missed family and home. On July 2, 1874, they returned to North America and after visiting Anna's family, bought a farm in Seville, Ohio. Here, for the first time, they had a home built to their specifications. Ceilings were 14½ feet tall; doors measured 8½ feet in length and were extra wide. All the furniture was built to their measurements. Martin had a special carriage and sleigh built for him and Anna so that they could travel in comfort. For the first time in their lives, it was others who felt out of proportion when they socialized. Dinner guests would have to be lifted onto dining room chairs, or climb up the rungs to seat themselves. The staff quarters were built to normal scale, as were the guest bedrooms.

Anna, wanting to spend time with children, took up teaching in the Sunday school at the First Baptist Church. Unable to sit comfortably in the church pew, Martin arranged to have one custom-made for Anna and him. As it turned out they needed the extra seating, for children flocked to them, climbing on the giants' laps, playing with the giants' gold watches, and getting candies out of the giants' pockets.

Life was good for Anna and Martin. Friends from their museum days would visit. The Dog-Faced Boy, the Living Skeleton, and especially close friends Elvira and Tom Thumb, dwarves who had met and married at Barnum's, were frequent guests. The Bates tended to socialize at home, especially after a dance floor in Seville had to be replaced when it collapsed under the weight of Anna and Martin.

The cost of the house and renovations had drained the family finances and Anna and Martin went on tour again. In 1878, they joined the W.W. Cole Circus as the "Tallest Man and Woman on the Face of the Earth — Each of Whom are (lacking only 1-3 inches) 8 Feet High." Anna and Martin did not stay long with the circus.

Anna was pregnant again. Feeling unwell and fearing the loss of a second baby, she and Martin returned home. There, on January 15, 1879, Anna went into labour — a labour that lasted 36 hours. At first, family Doctor A.P. Beach had attempted to deliver the baby alone. The head crowned, but

Giants

the baby remained firmly wedged by his shoulders.

Dr. Beach called for backup. He had Martin telegraph for Dr. J.D. Robinson at Wooster. Dr. Beach continued to try to manipulate the baby. He applied forceps, but none were available that were big enough for this baby's head, which measured 19 inches in circumference. In desperation, Dr. Beach and the recently arrived Dr. Robinson wrapped a bandage around the baby's neck and applied traction.

Slowly the baby emerged, first one shoulder and then the other. Shortly after midnight on January 19, 1879, Anna and Martin could finally look at their son. They held him and marvelled at him and called him simply "Babe." On the eleventh hour, he died.

At his autopsy, the baby was found to weigh 23 pounds and measure 28 inches in length. His chest circumference was 24 inches and his feet 5½ inches long. The medical record submitted the information to the *Guinness Book of World Records* as the largest baby ever born.

Anna and Martin both entered into a profound depression. They had had two children and both had died. They no longer had any hope that they could have healthy children in the future because Anna had a new health complication. She had been diagnosed with tuberculosis.

After several months' recuperation, Anna and Martin went on tour again, hoping to somehow relieve their anguish at the loss of their children. That summer they toured with the W.W. Cole Circus, returning home in the fall to spend the winter at the farm. As a special surprise for the children of Seville, Anna arranged to have a gigantic shoe made, much like the one from the "old woman who lived in a shoe" nursery rhyme. She and Martin filled the shoe with presents for the children. The next spring they again joined the Cole Circus, but this time they cut the tour short. Anna's health was deteriorating rapidly. She no longer had the stamina for such arduous travel.

On August 5, 1888, one day before her 42nd birthday, Anna died in her sleep. Martin found himself ordering a coffin to be made for her, rather than a birthday cake. But challenges caused by her size would again cause hardship and pain.

Martin had gone to a Cleveland, Ohio, company for the coffin rather than using the local carpenter. The company thought that the dimensions were a mistake, or a ridiculously roomy casket, and delivered one of normal size. Martin was beside himself with grief and rage. He wanted Anna to be treated with respect; instead, she lay in the parlour for three more days while another coffin was made and delivered. On the fourth day, the community gathered on the verandah to bid farewell to Anna, and then to bury her next to her son in the Mound Hill Cemetery. Martin, wishing to avoid the same mishap at his own death, ordered a second coffin made for himself. He and Anna had had a lifetime of dealing with the complications caused by their size.

Giants

Edouard Beaupre: The Saskatchewan Giant

On January 9, 1881, at Willow Bunch, Saskatchewan, close to the Montana border, the first of 20 children was born to Florestine Piché, the Métis wife of Gaspard Beaupre. Edouard weighed nine pounds, a large baby for a mother who was only five feet, four inches tall, but nothing indicated that he was to grow to be the tallest man in the world. Certainly no one in his small hometown could have predicted the bizarre path that his life was to take, or that his body would travel for 83 years after his death.

Willow Bunch was ranching country and young Edouard loved horses. At nine years of age he was six feet tall and a capable horseman. At age 15 he left school to follow his dream of becoming a cowboy. For two years he rode the range, but it was obvious to all, and especially to his horse, that Edouard would soon have to find a new career.

By the age of 17, Edouard weighed 300 pounds. At 7 feet 1 inch, his custom-made stirrups touched the ground. Cowboy work was out for Edouard, but he needed to work to help support his brothers and sisters. He was intelligent and though not able to write well, was fluent in four languages — French from his father, English from his neighbours, and Cree and Sioux from his mother's Native heritage. He was also gentle in nature — not suited for the life of a strong-man. When a child of the village had teased him, Edouard had picked up the child and gently placed him on the roof of a house, leaving him there until he promised not to tease.

Neighbours suggested that Edouard might have a future in the circus — this was an era of giants, and the story of Anna Swan of Cape Breton would have been heard even in Saskatchewan.

Edouard and two friends of his father's, Andre Gaudry and Albert Legare, set out to tour the big cities. They visited Winnipeg and Montreal. Enthralled by the response of the crowd, they set off through New York, Rhode Island, and Minnesota before they headed to California. On one of his train trips, Edouard caused a commotion when he was observed removing baggage from the overhead luggage rack without needing to stand.

One of his favourite acts was to lift a 700-pound horse to his shoulders. On a good night, he would carry the horse for a few steps in the ring, and then carry him back to his starting point and put him down on the ground. Before the trip was over, Edouard had acquired an agent. But he had also acquired something else — tuberculosis.

Despite his illness, the giant continued to grow. By 1902, at the age of 21, Edouard was 7 feet, 11 inches and weighed 365 pounds. The Ringling Brothers Circus took one look at him and fired their resident giant. A year later, he was 8 feet, 2½ inches, weighed close to 400 pounds, and had joined the Barnum & Bailey Circus. It took 23 yards of material to make him a suit.

The press loved Edouard and couldn't seem to take enough pictures of him. They photographed his size 26

The giant Edouard with a group of friends. The
woman standing in the picture is his
sister Josephine Beaupre.

shoes. They photographed a pair of his trousers — with a
man standing in each leg. They tried to photograph Edouard
head-on, but he would always turn his head away. When he
was 17, he'd had a bad fall from a horse and the right side of
his face was disfigured.

It was around this time that the press decided that
Edouard should get married to the American giant Ella

Ewing, of La Grange, Missouri. Ella was nine years older than Edouard and had never met him. But that didn't deter the press. Every two or three months they would announce their engagement. Each time, Edouard would deny his interest in getting married.

Edouard, like other giants, was phenomenally strong, but with time, the tuberculosis drained more and more of his strength. After each performance, he would find himself exhausted to the point of collapse, and yet his persistent cough prevented him from resting. The next day, he would perform again, never giving any hint of his illness. His family encouraged him to come home, but their poverty had not lessened and Edouard needed to work to support them. He continued performing with the Barnum & Bailey Circus and headed to the St. Louis World Fair with the rest of the troupe. It was while the circus was at the World Fair that Edouard died on July 3, 1904. He was only 23 years old.

The day of his death was unremarkable. At 11:45 on July 2, he finished his performance and sat down to have a cup of tea before going to bed. He began to cough, and spat up blood. Suddenly, he complained of a severe burning of his lungs. His friend J-H Noel tried to help him undress and get into bed, but Edouard was too weak. Noel later stated to the police that Edouard had said, " I am going to die." He asked for a glass of water, but when Noel returned with the water, he found Edouard unconscious. Noel called for an ambulance and Edouard was taken to the emergency hospital located on the exhibition grounds, where he died a few minutes later.

His story might have ended there, but the corpse of Edouard was to have a career of its own. For whatever reason, and there are several versions of the story, Edouard was not returned to Willow Bunch for burial. His father claimed that he had begun the trek to St. Louis to collect Edouard's body, but had been told that he would have to pay double to ship the body. He did not have sufficient money to do so and had agreed to donate the body for research. He said that the St. Louis doctors had promised to bury his son after they had completed their studies.

A second version stated that the corpse was returned to Edouard's agent, Aime Benard, who had him embalmed at great expense. Benard then asked the circus managers to pay the cost of shipping the body home to Willow Bunch, but they refused. By all accounts, there should have been more than enough money in Edouard's estate to pay the costs, but Edouard's savings had disappeared at the time of his death, along with his manager.

There is a third version of the story. A family member claimed that the St. Louis embalmers, Eberle and Keyes, 1110 Avenue, St. Ange, had said that the family had taken too long to collect the body and that they were seizing it.

The corpse of Edouard, which should have been on its way home for burial, was instead put on display. For a fee, St. Louis tourists could gaze at the body of the 23-year-old giant, who according to doctors was still growing at the time of his death.

For a year, Edouard's corpse made the rounds, first as an exhibit and then as a prop in a storefront window on Broadway near Market Street in the St. Louis commercial district. The police intervened and the corpse disappeared, only to reappear in a storefront window in East St. Louis. Again the police intervened and closed the exhibit. The corpse disappeared, only to show up again — this time in Canada. For six months in 1905, Edouard Beaupre's body stood in a sealed glass container in the Eden Museum of Montreal. The museum directors were, it appears, rather appalled by the number of people who turned out to view him, and closed the exhibit, selling or loaning Edouard to a circus.

Edouard's travels were not yet over. The circus went bankrupt and Edouard was abandoned and left to rot in a warehouse in Bellerive Park, Quebec. In 1907, children playing in the warehouse discovered Edouard's body. They called the police, who in turn called in a physician to inspect the remains. That physician notified Dr. Delorme, a professor of Medicine at the University of Montreal. Dr. Delorme paid $25 to have Edouard Beaupre's body transported to the university's anatomy department. Again Edouard seemed destined to be "studied." First Edouard was mummified by being treated with chemical preservatives that would keep his body intact for many years to come. Then the University of Montreal put Edouard Beaupre on display as the featured exhibit on university tours.

Giants

Edouard might still be there in his glass display case if it weren't for Dr. J. Maurice Blais. He wrote an article on Edouard that was published in the June 24, 1967 issue of *Canadian Medical Association Journal.* Dr. Blais had done his research, tracking down the St. Louis police reports of July 1904 and the newspaper clippings from the *St. Louis Daily Globe-Democrat.* While his journal article dealt primarily with the study of the pituitary gland, there was no mistaking the history or the identity of the corpse.

So it was that a medical student read the article, and eight years later, on a family visit home to Saskatchewan in 1975, told one of Edouard's relatives that Edouard resided at the University of Montreal. He happened to mention that Edouard was not even clothed and that anyone could look at him. The student added that a Quebec rock band had written a song about "le géant Beaupre" — a song that told of the wandering of the halls of the university by the ghost of Beaupre.

Ovila Lesperance, nephew to Edouard, had grown up hearing stories of the giant. He, like the rest of the family, believed that Edouard had been buried in a St. Louis cemetery. He reacted to the news with disbelief. Could it be possible that this Edouard Beaupre was the same Edouard that had died 69 years ago?

Aghast, Ovila headed to Montreal to retrieve Edouard's body and bring it home, but the university was unwilling to release him. They did offer a compromise. They would remove Edouard from public display, although his nude body would still be available to medical students. Lesperance insisted that a cloth be wrapped around Edouard's body within the case and then he returned home, seemingly defeated. He had the support of reporters who had picked up the story, but he felt powerless against the University of Montreal. How could an old man from Willow Bunch, Saskatchewan, fight the huge University of Montreal? They were insisting that Lesperance prove the legitimacy of his claim to the body in court.

For another 14 years, Edouard remained in his display case at the university, protected from photographers by a Quebec law making it illegal to photograph a corpse. In 1989, the university relented and finally agreed to release the body. There were certain conditions. The first was that the family would have to prove that they were legal next of kin. The second was that the university would agree to ship Edouard's ashes, but would not ship his body. Bernard Messier, head of the university's anatomy department, stated later in an article in *The Globe and Mail* that "maybe the moment [was] quite right if somebody [could] really prove he is a relative of Edouard Beaupre and that his intention is to bury him." He added, "We didn't want another freak show in Willow Bunch or anywhere else."

Cecile Gibouleau disputed the university's humanity. In that same January 9, 1990 article, *Globe and Mail* reporter Andre Picard quotes Beaupre's grandniece as saying, "there was fierce opposition within the university to giving up the body, and pressure from European museums that wanted to buy the body and put it on display."

Some felt that the university was being cheap — the cost of shipping such a huge corpse would have been expensive. The family stated that they had been told the body was so well embalmed that even if Edouard were buried, he would not decay. The fear was that grave robbers might snatch him.

On September 28, 1989, Edouard Beaupre was cremated. He was to have been buried on July 1, 1990, as part of a Canada Day Celebration, but instead the family waited until July 7. On that day, the ashes of the Saskatchewan giant were finally buried under the lawn at the Willow Bunch Museum. Some 400 people attended the ceremony, many of them relatives of Edouard Beaupre. It had taken him 86 years to come home.

Chapter 2
Witches

n 1484, Pope Innocent VIII instructed two Dominican monks to produce a "witch-hunter's" manual. *The Malleus Maleficarum* was intended to outline the signs and symptoms of witchcraft, describe torture techniques to gain confessions, and detail punishments for the guilty. During its term of usage, which lasted 250 years, many thousands of men and women were executed for witchcraft. Two of them were in Canada.

Daniel Voil: Witch or Political Pawn?
The fate of Daniel Voil was sealed years before his death. Whether he was a witch or not is unclear. What is known is that he had the misfortune to become a pawn in a battle for power and influence, a battle between the two highest pow-

ers of New France — Bishop Laval representing the church and Governor D'Avaugour representing the state.

Voil arrived in New France in 1659. Some said that he had sailed on the very ship that carried Bishop Laval, newly appointed head of the Catholic Church in New France. But Voil was not Catholic. Instead, he was of French Huguenot (Protestant) faith. Perhaps he had come to the attention of Bishop Laval onboard the ship, for it was recorded that Voil had renounced his Huguenot faith during the voyage from France and had taken on that of Catholicism. It may have been a true conversion, or it may have been based on practical considerations. Voil had learned that Huguenots were not well liked in the predominately Catholic New France and had been advised to abjure his faith if he wished employment.

Voil had done something else on that long journey from France. He had become infatuated with the beautiful Barbe Hallé — a Catholic, and the daughter of two fellow travellers. Voil had asked her parents for permission to marry the young girl, but was rejected. Both her parents felt that young Daniel was a man of "bad character." Was it his Huguenot background, or did they sense something truly evil in him?

New France in the middle of the seventeenth century was fraught with hardship and dangers. Religious intolerance was but one of these. Few of the habitants had been properly prepared for the harsh conditions of life they would find in this new land. In the winter, they contended with near starvation and the killing cold. For the rest of the year, they tried to eke a living from land so unlike the land they had previously known. The constant threat of Iroquois attack ensured that the habitants remained in a state of chronic anxiety. But the main problem, the overriding issue that would indirectly lead to Voil's death, was the ongoing sale of liquor to the Native peoples.

Since 1635, New France administrators had tried to control the problem. In addition to the countless rules they had imposed on the habitants regarding age of marriage, number of livestock permitted, and place of habitation, they had also imposed rules and punishments that related specifically to the sale of liquor.

The traders and trappers rebelled. They had come to New France to make their fortune, and the quickest way to do that was to barter the cheap and readily available rum for furs. Drunkenness, theft, and brawling continued to be a serious problem for the village of Quebec.

The state was determined to impose order on the unruly habitants and traders. At the same time, the Jesuits were also trying to gain influence over the habitants. When 26 Frenchmen defeated a party of 200 Iroquois, the Jesuits had declared it not a victory of superior firepower, but "a victory of the Queen of the Heavens." So much a part did both church and state play in the daily lives of the habitants, that each of the settler's cabins along the shore of the St. Lawrence above and below Quebec were supplied with a small iron cannon fabricated by the blacksmiths of the colony, and an image of the Virgin. It was said that if one did not save them, the other would.

Witches

While the habitants enjoyed a deep faith in their Catholicism and the power of religious miracles, they also retained their belief in magic and sorcery. When, in 1657, the Iroquois attacked a villager, cut off his head, and carried it home, the habitants had found no reason to dispute the story circulating about the incident. It was said and believed that on arriving at the Iroquois village the severed head had addressed the Natives in good Iroquois, "scolded them for his murder, and threatened them with divine vengeance." The Iroquois had scalped the head and disposed of the skull, hoping to silence the voice, but the voice was said to have continued uninterrupted.

It was amidst this scene of poverty, religious fervour, and mysticism that the Daniel Voil saga would unfold. When Voil had requested permission to marry Barbe Hallé, he had been refused. But that did not put an end to his infatuation with the beautiful young girl. Instead, it was rumoured that he had turned to witchcraft in his obsession to win Hallé.

Sister Marie de l'Incarnation, Superior of the Ursuline sisters, was one of those who accused him. In a letter she wrote to her son in September 1661, she said, "there are sorcerers and magicians in this country." One of those sorcerers she identified by name — Daniel Voil of Beauport, northeast of Quebec.

Marie de l'Incarnation then went on to explain the grounds for her accusation. Voil, she wrote, rejected by Barbe Hallé's parents, "sought to use the practices of Satan to achieve his ends." She charged that Voil first caused demons to appear in Hallé's home, and then apparitions that gave her no peace and caused her pain and terror. It was charged that an apparition of Voil appeared next, sometimes alone, sometimes in the company of friends. To add strength to the accusation of sorcery, it was pointed out that Barbe Hallé had no difficulty identifying these friends, even though she had never met them.

Barbe Hallé's family called upon the Jesuit brothers for assistance. Bishop Laval sent several of the priests to the Hallé home to try to dispel the demons, but there was no diminishment in activity. So the bishop himself set out for the house, intending to exorcise the demons. Amazingly, Bishop Laval was unsuccessful and the noise and disturbances escalated.

The sound of tambourines and flutes was heard. Stones "once firmly part of the wall became detached and flew through the air." And still the "Sorcerer Voil" and his friends tormented the girl's dreams.

In February 1661, Bishop Laval, "seeing that the demons were trying to tire him out by toil, and weary his patience by their buffooneries," had ordered that the miller and the girl be brought to Quebec. Barbe Hallé was placed in the convent of the Mother-Hospitallers. There, it was said, she told the sisters that Voil had appeared before her in the company of witches. She cried that he was trying to get her to marry him, but not before he had corrupted her. For her protection, the nuns would each night sew the girl into a sack. Each morning they would release her from the confining place.

Voil was thrown into prison on suspicion of being a "relapsed heretic, a blasphemer and a profaner of the sacraments." Bishop Laval was determined to do away with Voil — the man had made a fool of him. First, he had become a Catholic, and then he had renounced this faith and become a heretic once more. He'd "haunted" a young woman, causing all manner of strange occurrences in her home. The Jesuit brothers had proved powerless against him, and even Bishop Laval himself, the highest officer of the Catholic Church in New France, had been unequal to his evil sorcery. Bishop Laval was intent on gaining influence in New France, not in losing it — especially not through the machinations of a Huguenot.

Bishop Laval visited the recently appointed Governor D'Avaugour. He spoke eloquently of the damage done by the trade in liquor with Native peoples. He derided the wanton behaviour of the habitants, and then ended his audience with the governor by requesting the death penalty for those engaged in the "abhorred traffic." The new governor, hoping perhaps to conciliate the Jesuits after years of acrimonious relations between them and the previous governor, permitted the decree to take effect.

After eight months of captivity on the original charges of blasphemy, heresy, and sacrilege, Voil was sentenced to death for "being found guilty of trafficking in spirits with the Indians." The fact that Daniel Voil was by all accounts a miller, not a fur trader, seemed unimportant, as was the lack of evidence that he had ever engaged in the barter of fur for liquor.

On October 7, 1661, Voil was taken out of his cell and executed by arquebus. The habitants all believed that he was executed for sorcery, not illegal trade.

Governor D'Avaugour recognized that he had been outmaneuvered in the battle between state and church for authority. Whatever his feelings toward Daniel Voil, he saw his execution as a clear indication that Bishop Laval was once again meddling with civil authority. The governor retaliated in the most harmful way he could, a way that would disturb Bishop Laval more than any other action he could take, a way that would teach Bishop Laval the consequences of meddling with civil matters. D'Avaugour declared "that henceforth there is full license to sell liquor to the Indians." Voil's execution resulted in the effective legitimization of the barter of fur for liquor. Bishop Laval must surely have thought that only a sorcerer could have brought about this end.

It is not known what became of Barbe Hallé after Voil was executed. Did she return home or did she remain in the convent, sewed into her sack each night? Death, it is supposed, would have little effect on a sorcerer's influence.

Bishop Laval continued to fight the powers of sorcery and witchcraft. Two years after Voil's death, a Ville Marie (Montreal) tribunal convicted Rene Besnard of casting a spell of impotence over his former girlfriend's husband Pierre Gadois. Bishop Laval annulled the still-barren marriage of

Gadois and his wife Marie Pontonnier on the grounds of "permanent impotence caused by witchcraft."

Marie-Josephe Corriveau: Witch or Innocent Victim?
On May 14, 1733, an exquisite baby girl was born in the village of Saint-Vallier, New France. Before her 30th birthday, she would die on the gallows, convicted of murder and suspected of witchcraft and sorcery.

Her name was Marie-Josephe, daughter of Joseph and Marie Corriveau. Her mother was a descendent of the *filles du roi* — orphans brought over from France as brides for the habitants. Her parents were not rich, but they owned fertile farmland on the south shore of the St. Lawrence River opposite Quebec, the capital of New France. Situated as it was, the farm commanded a view of the Isle d'Orleans — an island known to be inhabited by sorcerers and a place where a coven of witches was said to hold its festivals.

Marie-Josephe's childhood was uneventful. She was the adored and very beautiful only child of a young mother and a much older father. At the age of 16, she married the handsome and wealthy farmer Charles Bouchard. People from miles around attended at the parish church to wish the couple well.

The marriage seemed to prosper, and though they had no children the couple appeared to their neighbours to be happy. But on the morning of April 17, 1760, people were amazed to see Marie-Josephe running from her house to the village centre. She was distraught, weeping, beside herself. She said, between sobs, that she had awoken that morning to find her husband dead beside her.

The people of Saint-Vallier couldn't do enough for Marie-Josephe. They imagined her terror on awakening beside the cooling corpse of Charles. They imagined her leaning over to kiss his brow, and her shock at finding it cold.

They decided that it would be best for Marie-Josephe if they had a quick burial. The widow was so distraught, they said, that it would do nothing but harm to delay the process. So, within a space of two days, they had held the funeral and buried Charles in the parish cemetery, beside the church. They then comforted Marie-Josephe as best they could, though little seemed to help.

When, less than three months later, Marie-Josephe married again, the habitants worried that she had been hasty, had perhaps acted out of sorrow and loneliness. Her new husband, Louis Dodier, was a drinker known to frequent the taverns and socialize with the British troops who had been garrisoned in the area since the British had successfully fought off the forces of the Chevalier de Levis.

The gossips of the parish spread rumours about Marie-Josephe. They questioned whether it was seemly for a widow to marry again so soon. Of course, at 27 she was no longer young, they said, and could not afford to be choosy, but three months was far less than a respectable mourning period.

Again there were no children, but the couple seemed

content. Marie-Josephe had her father living next door and he provided her company when her husband was at the tavern. Everything changed on Monday, January 27, 1763. That day dawned cold, so cold that people delayed going to their barns to feed their animals. When the Dodier stableman had finally made his way to the stable, he found the corpse of Louis Dodier in his horse's stall. It appeared that Dodier had been kicked in the head and had probably died instantly from the terrible wound.

The stableman ran to the house to tell Marie-Josephe. She immediately sent him on to the barracks to report the death and fetch the priest. The captain of the militia, the priest Father Thomas Blondeau, and 10 others descended on the barn where Marie-Josephe and her father stood vigil over Dodier's body. After a cursory examination, the captain of the militia reported that Louis Dodier had died as a result of a kick to the head. Major Abercrombie granted permission for an immediate burial.

A week later, suspicions surfaced. The authorities questioned Joseph Corriveau's servant girl. Had she seen or heard anything unusual, they asked? The frightened girl, Isabelle Sylvain, responded that she had woken and heard yelling from the stable the night of Louis Dodier's death — and a sound as if a horse was being beaten.

In light of this new evidence, Governor James Murray granted permission for an exhumation of the body. Dodier was dug up and taken to the barracks for an autopsy. This time the examination was thorough, and the army surgeon declared that the gash on the farmer's head was four inches deep, far too deep to be made by a horse, even one with shoes on, such as Dodier's horse. To add credence to his suspicion, the injury was clear of any trace of manure or straw. Both would have been imbedded in the cut if a horse had dealt the killing blow.

The army surgeon had seen many a battlefront injury. He suspected that an axe, not a horse, had caused the fatal blow and he reported those findings to Major Abercrombie, who ordered the militia to return to the Corriveau and Dodier homes. They were to question everyone again — especially the stableman and the servant girl.

The militia was familiar with Dodier from his visits to the tavern frequented by the English. They also knew that Joseph adored his only child. Had Joseph and Dodier fallen into an argument over Dodier's drinking and his treatment of Marie-Josephe?

The militia first questioned Isabelle, Joseph's servant girl. Her bedroom was close to the stairs and her window overlooked the shared stable yard. She said that she had heard Marie-Josephe go down to the stable and then come back into the house and speak with her father. Isabelle said that Marie-Josephe and her father had then returned to the stable together. It now seemed that both the Corriveaus — father and daughter — were implicated in Dodier's murder.

As Quebec was then under British rule, the English

military governor James Murray served as the civil authority for the township. Governor Murray charged Joseph Corriveau with the murder of his son-in-law Louis Dodier and had him placed in the military jail. Marie-Josephe was charged as an accomplice in the murder. The military barracks was an unsuitable place for a female prisoner, so Governor Murray had an escort of soldiers take Marie-Josephe across the ice-filled St. Lawrence River to the Ursuline Convent in Quebec, where she would await trial.

For two months Marie-Josephe lived at the Ursuline Convent — both as a prisoner and a houseguest. On Tuesday, March 29, a court martial (the only tribunal existing in the country at the time) was held in the reception room of the convent. Joseph Corriveau was brought from the military barracks and his daughter was escorted from her room.

The court martial began. First, the stableman testified to finding Dodier dead in the barn. Then the army surgeon took the stand and spoke to his findings regarding the likely cause of death. Next came the servant girl Isabelle with her damning evidence. It appeared that Marie-Josephe and her father would both be found guilty and sentenced to death.

But Joseph Corriveau spoke out. In a loud voice he claimed that he, and he alone, had dealt the blow that had killed Louis Dodier. And so it was that on April 10, 1763, less than three months after the murder, the tribunal sentenced him to hang for the murder of his son-in- law.

Marie-Josephe would not escape unpunished for what

many felt was her complicity in her husband's murder. They reasoned that if she had not been involved, she would have reported her husband missing when he failed to return home that night.

Her proposed punishment was harsh. The military court sentenced her to receive 60 lashes on bare skin from a cat-of-nine tails, not once but at three separate locations. The whippings were to be held in public at the place of hanging of her father, at the marketplace in Quebec, and in the parish of St. Vallier. It was suggested that she also be branded with a hot iron — branded with the letter M for her part in the murder of her husband. The tribunal had not believed her father's protestations of Marie-Josephe's innocence.

Marie-Josephe was escorted back to her room at the convent to await her flogging. Her father was hustled back to his cell at the garrison. There, a soldier summoned the Jesuit Reverend Father Glapion to receive the prisoner's confession. It wasn't long before Joseph's courtroom confession began to dissemble. Joseph was willing to die for his daughter, but he wasn't willing to lie to his confessor. He told the priest the truth — that he had had no part in his son-in-law's death, and that his daughter had been the one to swing the axe.

The priest informed the militia and a new trial was ordered. Five days later, on April 15, 1763, Marie-Josephe again stood in the convent reception room, charged with the murder of her husband. No more was there any mention of her being simply an accomplice. This time she stood alone,

Witches

and no one came to her aid.

Three days later, a month shy of her 30th birthday, Marie -Josephe was hanged on the Plains of Abraham. A large crowd had been expected to gather for the execution of a woman found guilty of murdering her husband, but rumours had begun to spread fear amongst the people.

It was said that Marie-Josephe had often looked across the waters from her home on the south shore to the Isle d'Orleans, where it was known that sorcerers lived. It was said that Marie-Josephe's mother had often taken her to the island as a child, had taken her across the river on nights of the full moon to dance with the coven of witches that practised their arts there. It was said that not only was she a witch, but that she was the daughter of a witch, and that her grandmother had been the daughter of an alchemist of Old France.

Marie-Josephe had enemies and they fanned the rumours. People from the parish who had once supported her, even comforted her, now took fault with the haste of her actions in remarrying. Those same people who had recommended the hasty burial of her first husband Charles now conveniently forgot that it was they who had suggested it and fed the lie that Marie-Josephe had insisted on the quick burial. It was a short step from there to imply that Marie-Josephe had murdered her first husband, too.

Once admired and adored, Marie-Josephe was now depicted as a heartless and cruel murderer, a witch who was a member of the coven that met on the Isle d'Orleans. No one but the most curious or the most foolish attended the hanging, for the parishioners knew that a dying witch had power — the power to curse those who witnessed her death.

Marie-Josephe's humiliation was to be complete. After her execution she was cut down, and a cage of iron was forged around her body. The soldiers then lifted the cage onto a farm wagon and transported it and its burden across the river to Point Levis. At the intersection of the four roads, the soldiers suspended the cage from a tree, leaving the dead woman inside as a warning to those who had murder or witchcraft in their hearts.

Marie-Josephe's corpse slowly rotted, exposed as it was to the spring rains and the harsh sun. Birds poked their beaks through the iron bars, tearing strips of flesh off the lifeless body. Rats climbed up the tree, onto the ropes, and into the cage.

The curious stayed away, fearing reprisals from Marie-Josephe. It was said that the intersection was haunted. Accidents were frequent. It was as if people were unable to concentrate when they reached that spot in the road. Walkers said they felt the claws of skeletal hands grasping their neck if they lingered too long, that they heard a woman's voice demanding to be carried across the waters to the Isle d'Orleans so that she could dance with the Devil.

On May 25, 1763, Marie-Josephe's cage was cut down. No one claimed responsibility. Perhaps it was soldiers, armed as they were, who braved the phantom. Perhaps it was the villagers together with a priest, who wanted to put Marie-

A statue of the infamous witch La Corriveau
by sculptor Alfred Laliberté

Josephe's soul to rest. The cage was transported to the cemetery, where a pit was dug and Marie-Josephe's remains were laid to rest still held within the cage.

That might have been the end of the story. But in 1830, a cemetery worker preparing a burial site had dug up the unmarked grave and discovered the cage of La Corriveau, as she was now called. The cage was sold to the Barnum

& Bailey Circus in New York, where it was displayed to the horror and delight of the patrons. Some say that the cage was sold again, others that it was destroyed in the fires at Barnum's. La Corriveau's spirit is said to sweep through the skies on at least four days of the year: the Witches' Sabbath (April 30), Walpurgisnacht (May 1), Halloween (October 31), and All Souls' Day (November 2). On these days it is said that you might feel the cold claws of La Corriveau's skeletal fingers on your neck

Chapter 3
Conjurers and Wizards

he Native peoples of Canada have skilled conjurers and medicine men among them, shamans who can communicate with their spirit guides. When the settlers of the seventeenth and eighteenth centuries came to Canada, they brought with them their own beliefs in wizardry and witchcraft. Often these beliefs lived side by side in harmony, but on occasion, one belief system would set out to discredit the other.

The Shaking Tent
In July 1609, Samuèl de Champlain wrote in his journal that members of his army — the Huron, Algonquin, and Montagnais — lacked discipline and demonstrated

"unsoldierly habits," even when in Iroquois enemy territory. Champlain couldn't understand why his Native allies refused to post a sentry at night. The warriors responded that they had no need of sentries, that their shaman would receive word of danger from the spirits who spoke with him during the shaking tent ceremony.

Not reassured, Champlain became the first of many who sought to study and discredit the shaking tent ceremony. Over the next 300 years, soldiers, missionaries, explorers, and traders would make many attempts to expose the shaking tent ceremony as a fake, but none would ever be successful. The mystery of the shaking tent remains unsolved to this day. While the ceremony defies rational explanation, time and again it has brought knowledge to participants that could not have been obtained through any other source.

In his desire to invalidate the ritual, Champlain observed several shaking tent ceremonies. He knew that the Native peoples placed great faith in the ceremony — that they used it to consult with their spirit guides or to heal their sick. On many occasions, Champlain watched the men erect the teepee, or tent, and saw the shaman enter. He listened to the eerie moans and cries that came from within the teepee, saw the teepee vibrate, and on occasion even witnessed sparks fly out of the top of the structure. But he remained convinced that there was trickery involved. The trouble was, he had been unable to observe what form that trickery took. Worse, he could not deny the accuracy of the predictions that would result from the ceremony.

Father Paul Le Jeune was next in a long line of doubt-ers to study the tent. He had arrived in Quebec from France in 1632, intent on converting the Natives to Catholicism. He had soon realized that his attempts to convert the Natives to his chosen belief were thwarted by the shamans, who were equally intent on preserving their own Native spirituality. Father Le Jeune, head of the Jesuit Mission to the Hurons, was a man with a cause. He was determined to use all the education and training given to him by the Jesuit fathers to study and discredit the practice of the shaking tent, and with it, the shamans.

Father Le Jeune believed in miracles and visions — his faith depended on them. However, he only recognized those miracles and visions performed within the Catholic faith community. Anything else he credited to the interference and influence of the Devil. Father Le Jeune had heard enough about the ceremony to know what to expect. He was deter-mined to prove that the sounds coming from the tent were the result of ventriloquism, that the movement of the tent was simply the result of trickery, and that the oracles were nothing but guesswork.

In 1634, he recorded his eyewitness account of his first shaking tent ceremony. First, he wrote, the men took six poles and pushed them deep into the ground in the form of a circle. At the top they placed a large ring to keep the poles together. Then they covered the structure with blankets, leaving an opening or vent at the top

Le Jeune observed a young shaman turn back a flap of the blanket and enter the teepee, then lower the flap behind him. Soon a moan was heard — it was soft at first, but then rose to a complaining note. Next a whistle was heard, as if from far away. Then was heard a cry like that of an owl, then the howl of a wolf and the sound of singing. The teepee began to shake. At first it was just a vibration but then the movement became so violent that Father Le Jeune feared the structure would collapse. For three hours the teepee shook, sometimes swaying to and fro, at other times bending its top down towards the earth.

Testing the poles, Father Le Jeune saw that they were still solidly embedded in the ground. For all his belief that the shaman was using some sort of trickery, Father Le Jeune could not see how it was done. He voiced astonishment that even if it were trickery, how could one man have the strength to move the tent for more than three continuous hours?

Father Le Jeune derided the Natives, calling out that the shaman would surely die of exhaustion if allowed to continue. He was rebuked by Manitou-Chat-Che (a previous lapsed convert of Father Le Jeune's) and was told to be quiet, for the "soul of our medicine man has now left his body, and has risen to the top of the teepee. It is hovering there to reach the spirits."

Suddenly there was a cry of excitement and Father Le Jeune looked up to see fiery sparks issuing from the vent hole.

Conjurers and Wizards

The excitement increased as people directed the shaman to "call the others." The shaman responded in a harsh voice, different from that of his own. A drum began to sound among the gathered — the sparks signified that the spirits were arriving and soon the shaman would be able to consult them on matters important to his people.

In turn they asked questions of the Great Spirit. They were told that the shaman would survive the winter, but that his wife would die, that there would be little snow, and that there would be moose for hunting but at a considerable distance away.

Le Jeune discredited it all and attempted to speak to the shaman when he exited the tent, but the priest saw no one. Angry at La Jeune's lack of respect, Manitou-Chat-Che challenged the priest to enter the tent, claiming, "You will see for yourself, Black Robe, that your body will remain below, while your soul will rise up on high." Father Le Jeune refused the offer, convinced that trickery existed, but at a loss as to how it had been done.

The explorer Alexander Henry the Elder recorded the next real challenge to the existence of the shaking tent in 1764. Henry was in Sault Ste. Marie when a deputation from Sir William Johnson — the Chief Indian Agent of the British in North America — arrived at the Ojibwa settlement. Sir William wished the Ojibwa to dine with him at Fort Niagara on Lake Ontario in order to sign a peace treaty with the English.

The Ojibwa were understandably hesitant, fearing a

trap. Henry, desperate to return south, was encouraging, so the Ojibwa decided to consult Mikinak — the Great Turtle. He, they said, would tell them the true intent of the British.

Henry asked if he could observe the ceremony. He took meticulous notes. First, he said, they constructed a large wigwam, and inside that, constructed a smaller one measuring approximately four feet in diameter. The construction was notably sturdy, the frame being made of five poles ten feet long and eight inches in diameter. Each pole was of a different wood and was set two feet deep into the ground. Over the frame were draped moose hides that were fastened tightly to the poles with thongs of hide.

Once it was dark, the shaman entered the tent. "His head was scarcely inside when the edifice began to shake; and the skins were no sooner let fall than the sounds of the numerous voices were heard, and beneath them, some yelling, some barking like dogs, some howling like wolves; and in this horrible concert were mingled screams and sobs, as of despair, anguish and the sharpest pain."

There was silence and then "a low and feeble voice, resembling the cry of a young puppy was heard." This, it transpired, was the voice of Mikinak. Henry was told that the previous sounds — the barking and the howling — had been the voices of evil spirits.

With offerings of tobacco, the chief requested that Mikinak act as a mediator with the good spirits and ask whether the English were intending to attack the Ojibwa.

A second question had followed the first: are there many redcoats at Fort Niagara? Henry observed the tent shake violently — it appeared as if it would fall to the ground. Then a piercing cry rent the air and all was silent.

Eventually the shaman exited the tent. He reported that Mikinak had visited Fort Niagara, where he had observed "no great number of redcoats." But, he added, Mikinak had reported that the St. Lawrence River at Montreal was covered with boats — all of them filled with redcoats and guns. It would be safe to visit Sir William though. Mikinak had prophesied that every man would return home safe again. Henry watched the tent until midnight, as he was intent on finding evidence of fraud. There was none that he could find.

On July 28, 1848, Paul Kane, artist and explorer, camped with Cree voyageurs at Dog's Head, Manitoba. He asked whether anyone had looked into the tent during a ceremony and was told that "a man had once had the temerity to peep under the covering which enclosed the tent but that he got such a fright that he never fairly recovered from it, nor could he ever be prevailed to tell what it was that had so appalled him."

By the mid 1800s, an explorer, a priest, a trader, and an artist-explorer had tried to learn the mystery behind the shaking tent — to no avail. In 1920, two men would join ranks to try to disprove the magic of the tent. One of them was a Hudson Bay Company (HBC) factor, identified only by his initials, E.B. The other was a corporal in the RCMP — also unidentified. Both were posted to Northern Manitoba, in a community made up primarily of Native people whose reserve lay along the shoreline of a lake.

It was clear from E.B.'s account that he had not the slightest belief in the ability of the shamans. In fact, he began his account by stating that the RCMP, the HBC, and the Catholic missionaries held shamans in low regard and used every opportunity to discredit them and their powers.

One day, a situation arose that seemed made to order. A young man from another community had travelled to the village to seek a wife. Either through her influence, or his own wishes, the man decided that he would like to settle in the village and that he wanted to take on the title of shaman.

The resident shaman, a revered elder, had shown no inclination to give up his coveted position. So the young stranger challenged the shaman, claiming that his magic was stronger than that of the old man. Such a brazen claim was soon all over the reserve, and came to the attention of the RCMP corporal. The opportunity to discredit both the newcomer and the elder seemed too good to be true.

The corporal determined to pit the two against each other — the brash young stranger and the elder. He invited the HBC factor to attend and witness the humiliation of the two shamans.

The young man built the migawap, a northern Manitoba-style teepee. He first took four poplar poles, each 20 feet in length, and bound them firmly together at the top. At the base he roped each pole to a tree. He then covered the frame with canvas, leaving a small opening at the apex. The corporal and the factor, together with the members of the community, tested the strength of the structure. They pulled on the poles, they pushed on them, but nothing would move them. How, they wondered, could they test the motion within the tent? They took a tin can, placed pebbles in it, and hung it from a long leather thong lowered through the apex. The migawap was complete.

The corporal and the factor stood watch while the people gathered in the light of the full moon. It seemed the entire community had come to watch the competition.

At the time set for the contest, the young man and the elder shaman approached, followed by the chief in full ritual regalia. The corporal and the factor, sure of their success and the brilliance of their plan, stationed themselves so that between them, they could see all sides of the migawap.

The young man invited the elder to go first, to do his best to rattle the stones in the can hanging suspended in the tent. The elder began his dance. He sang and chanted, he called upon the spirits to shake the tent and make the stones rattle. Only silence and stillness greeted him. The constable and the factor were enthused. This was working out exactly as they had planned. As soon as they had humiliated the young man, they could once and for all put to rest the superstitions that they had fought so hard to vanquish.

The young man stepped forward. He began his chant, his feet started to move in his pattern. After only a few minutes, the tent began to vibrate though the man kept at least three feet away from the migawap as decreed by the constable. The sound of the stones rattling in the can was clear, sounding even above the noise of the onlookers who sensed a clear victor in the contest.

The corporal had been watching the migawap the entire time. He had seen no one enter, but it was clear to him that some trickery must be involved. He unsheathed his hunting knife, strode up to the tent, slit the canvas open in one long tear, and looked inside, sure of his victory.

Victory was not to be his that day. The tent was empty and the young man, clear winner in the contest between himself and the old shaman, was pronounced victorious. The RCMP corporal and the HBC factor joined the long list of people who had failed to discredit the shaking tent ceremony.

Dr. Troyer and the Baldoon Mystery

In 1793, the first permanent white settler, Dr. John Troyer, arrived at Long Point, Ontario. That summer he built himself a log home, and then planted an apple orchard on the 15 acres of flat land along the sheltered shore of Long Point Bay on Lake Erie. With time, his skill as a farmer would garner him much praise, but it was his pathological hatred of witches and his efforts to catch them that would make him famous and earn him the title of "the Witch Hunter of Long Point." One particular case — that of the Baldoon haunting — would ensure him a permanent place in Canadian history of occultism.

Conjurers and Wizards

Dr. Troyer was not in fact a doctor at all. He was, however-er, a skilled blacksmith, an excellent shot, and a good farmer. On top of these skills, he added those of dentistry, healing, and an encyclopedic knowledge of herbal remedies. He was the closest thing to a physician that the future community would have.

Although Troyer had left his Mennonite community in Pennsylvania to come north, he nevertheless decorated his log cabin with traditional Mennonite hex signs to ward off the "dark-eyed evil temptress." Over the lintel of his door, he hung upside-down horseshoes to prevent witches from entering the premises. Troyer next built a palisade and placed six small cannons on its periphery — cannons he had brought with him from Pennsylvania. Initially, Troyer feared maraud-ing groups of Native people, but it was not long before his fear of them was overshadowed by his fear of witches.

Yet Troyer, for all his stated loathing of witches, was known to engage in the "black arts" himself. He performed incantations to raise evil spirits, and claimed that he was knowledgeable about the unseen world. Troyer blamed the witches of his community for any ills that befell him and oth-ers. He was as likely to blame a sickness on the "bewitching" of a person as he was to blame a disease. In time he began to hear stories of the strange goings-on at Baldoon, Ontario, of a farmer tormented by an evil spirit. Troyer was convinced that a witch was at the root of the trouble, but he had not yet been asked to help. That time would come, he predicted.

To protect himself while he slept, Troyer placed a bear trap at the foot of his bed and bolted it to the floor. The "witch trap" was huge, its jaws measuring 90 centimetres in length and 76 centimetres in height — big enough, Troyer felt, to hold even the most powerful witch. Despite these precautions, Troyer told his neighbours, the witches had evaded the trap one night and had taken him from his bed. He said that they had transformed him into a horse and had ridden him across Lake Erie to Dunkirk to attend a coven of witches. On arrival at Dunkirk, he said that he had been tied to a hitching post, made to eat rye straw, and forced to watch the witches as they danced. So exhausted was Troyer by this kidnapping that he had been ill for weeks after.

Still, his witch-hunting skills were in high demand in the 1830s. Troyer lived in an area of Ontario settled by dispossessed Highland Scots, who brought to Canada their beliefs in witches, the little people, and spectres. While they would have had their own remedies for witches' spells, they consulted Troyer when their counter spells didn't work. He was in an odd position — consulted by the settlers, but ostracized by them too, for they considered his obsession with witches a "peculiar mental malady."

Troyer had garnered a great deal of respect for his skill in animal husbandry and human healing. Nevertheless, people feared him and were reluctant to appear on friendly terms with him, in case they were seen to be like him. The events surrounding his son Michael's return from the dead added to

Conjurers and Wizards

the mystique surrounding Troyer. When Michael was a young man, he fell into a deep coma. For three days and nights he lay in bed, unresponsive to voice or touch. His body was warm, though cooler than normal, and he seemed to have no heartbeat. His friends made plans for the burial. They made a coffin and took it to the Troyer house. When they got there, Michael had recovered and was fully conscious. Such a miraculous recovery deserved respect for the healer. But it also raised question as to the source of his abilities.

In 1831, Troyer was finally asked to deal with the haunting at the McDonald farm in Baldoon. Troyer and McDonald had been on a seemingly parallel course for two years. Each had been aware of the other. Troyer was aware of the trouble McDonald was experiencing, but had not been asked to help. McDonald was aware of Troyer's reputation, but had resisted seeking his help. After all, wasn't Troyer the man who raised the dead? Didn't McDonald have enough trouble on his hands without involving a man with a reputation like that? Finally, fear overcame caution, and now McDonald stood before Troyer. He told him the story in great detail, recounting the happenings as if they had occurred yesterday ...

The trouble started in the late fall of 1829, when several young girls were in John McDonald's barn, plaiting straw into summer hats. With no warning, a crossbeam fell and landed amidst the girls. Within a short time, a second and then a third fell. The girls, thoroughly frightened, left the barn and went into the house, but the strange happenings followed them.

A bullet crashed through the window and fell to the floor. Then came a second and a third bullet. The girls were not injured, but were frightened and ran to a neighbour's house. When McDonald returned home from his fields, he found three of his windows broken and lead bullets scattered on the floor of his parlour. He was not terribly surprised by the happenings — he'd been expecting them.

McDonald and his wife had been dealing with mettle-some occurrences since the summer. Several times, they had been woken by the sound of many men marching through their house. Each time, McDonald had gone to investigate the source of the noise, but had found nothing. Now, standing in the shambles of his parlour, he knew there was no point in looking for a logical explanation for the bullets. The area around his house was flat and marshy, not a location likely to be hit by a misplaced hunter's bullet.

Time passed and the bullets kept coming — even when people were stationed around the house to watch for trickery. The shells would start flying every day at about 3 p.m. and continue until nightfall. McDonald nailed boards across the broken glass, but still the bullets penetrated the house, though they made no mark on the boards. On one particular day, James Johnson, a young neighbour, collected several "witch balls" in his cap and took them home to show his mother. She, however, would not allow them in the house, fearing that "the witches would come and take James with them."

After a week or two, pebbles, and then stones, replaced the bullets. One neighbour, Neil Campbell was struck on the chest. Convinced that the whole thing was an ornate fraud, he challenged the "thing" to throw another stone. A second, larger stone sailed through the window, hitting him with such force that he was winded. Campbell picked up the stone and hurled it into the river that ran beside the house. Back came the rock, wet and muddy.

Baldoon began to attract people who thought they could put an end to the goings on at McDonald's house. Reverend Alexander Brown of the Methodist Church in Chatham came to see if he could be of any help. Stones continued to come through the window. In front of 30 people, Brown marked the stones as they came into the house, and then threw them into the river. The stones came flying back, their marks still clearly visible on their now wet surfaces. Brown then placed several of the wet stones in a leather shot bag, tied it shut, and hung it in the chimney piece. The stones came flying back through the window and when Brown retrieved the bag from the chimney, he found it empty.

McDonald considered consulting Troyer at that time, but he was a God-fearing man and knew that Troyer was a dabbler in the black arts. So instead, he decided to continue to seek assistance from clergy.

In the spring of 1830, he requested that an itinerant Baptist preacher by the name of Harmon conduct a prayer meeting at his house. McDonald reasoned that whatever was haunting the house would leave once the meeting began. Instead, the presence of the clergyman and the conducting of a service seemed to present a challenge to whatever it was that was tormenting the house and its occupants.

As Pastor Harmon stood up to conduct a prayer, a rock burst through a panel of the door and rolled across the floor in front of him. Then a shower of pebbles fell on the gathered congregation. It was as if the pebbles were raining right through the ceiling of the room.

That spring and summer, McDonald noticed that his crops were growing poorly and that his livestock seemed to get ill more frequently. He began to wonder if he had been "bewitched" — if he was the victim of someone's witchcraft. McDonald had little patience with those who spoke of witches and spells. Nevertheless, he took the precaution of nailing an upside down horseshoe over the lintel of his door. He didn't think it would make any difference but he felt he had to try every avenue.

Unfortunately, this seemed only to increase the frequency of the torments. Fire was now added to the arsenal. On a regular basis, a small coal of fire, about the size of a hickory nut, would drop in any part of the house, and a flame would kindle instantly. Nothing seemed immune from the fire spook. Clothing, bundles of flax, and even closets would instantaneously burst into flame. In one day, 50 separate outbreaks of fire were recorded.

McDonald ordered that no fires were to be lit in the

house — for any reason. The cooking of meals and the heating of water would be done in his father Daniel's house. But fires still broke out. During harvest, McDonald's father's barn caught fire. As the community rushed to put out the flames, a new fire started at John McDonald's house.

In despair, McDonald appealed to the Catholic priest to conduct an exorcism of his house. He had tried the Methodist church and he had tried the Baptist church — perhaps the Catholics knew something that they didn't. For a week the priest lived in McDonald's house, sprinkled holy water in every room, and recited prayers. These efforts were of no use. Finally, the priest suggested that the happenings must be a punishment for some sin committed by a member of the family. McDonald threw the priest out.

Next, an amateur psychical investigator named Robert Barker paid McDonald a visit. The man had come all the way from Michigan to inform McDonald that an evil spirit plagued his house. He offered to ban the spirit using an ancient ritual he had discovered in a book on occultism and witchcraft.

McDonald accepted the offer and watched Barker get to work. First Barker made a large placard and nailed it to the front door of the farmhouse. On the placard he had written, "I commend you, troublesome spirits, to leave this house, in the name of the Father, the Son and the Holy Ghost."

But soon after the placard was mounted, things turned sour. The Windsor police were that day investigating the goings-on at Baldoon. They had arrived in the village to hear talk of an American stranger who was knowledgeable of spells and charms, and who was presently carrying out some sort of ceremony at the house.

Police officer Constable George Burnshaw consulted with the local magistrate. He was told that he had grounds to arrest Barker because it was a criminal offence to "pretend to any kind of witchcraft, conjuring, or fortune telling." Constable Burnshaw obtained a warrant and set out to arrest Barker. At first, the American managed to evade authorities by hiding in a barn, but he was caught and arrested the following day. It was six months before friends in the U.S. were able to get him released.

The situation got much worse in the fall of 1830. It was at that point that Thomas Babison, a neighbour of McDonald's, saw the McDonald house rock on its foundations as if shaken by an earthquake. In turn, each of the four corners of the house tilted up, exposing the underside of the floorboards. Soon after, the house erupted in flames, and was severely damaged. McDonald lost nearly everything, and yet he still did not know why he was the victim. He didn't even know what he was a victim of. He sensed that whatever "it" was, was truly evil. But still he was afraid to seek help from Troyer. Hadn't the police arrested Barker for pretending to be a witch-hunter? What would they do to McDonald if he hired someone that everyone knew was a true witch-hunter?

Neighbouring families took in one or two of McDonald's

children, but soon asked them to leave, as the happenings seemed to follow wherever they went. The family next moved in with McDonald's father Daniel, but illness soon fell on his farm, too. Healthy oxen dropped dead while ploughing the fields, hogs became ill and died, and hens were found dead in the chicken house. Fearful of bringing more doom on his father's house, McDonald borrowed old sails from a fisherman neighbour and made a tent in which he and the older children lived for the summer months. On the third day of his tent existence, his second barn burned to the ground, and with it, his grain harvest for the year. His family faced famine.

Desperate, McDonald approached other spiritualists for help. He called in a Native medicine man who told him there was no doubt he was the victim of witchcraft. The man told McDonald that he would put a stop to the trouble. He dug a large hole under a tree and placed a kettle in it. He then performed an incantation that he said would cause the evil spirit to come from the house and enter the kettle. As he prepared to leave, the medicine man said he would return later to dig up the kettle and cart the witch away. The hole was dug, the kettle buried, and McDonald waited to be free of the witchcraft. But the medicine man never returned, and McDonald was unwilling to risk digging up the kettle himself.

McDonald now became fixated on the idea that a witch was causing the problems. That was what the American psychic had told him, and that was what the Native medicine man had said. He decided to determine who the witch could be, and before long had settled on the identity of the most likely candidate. It was the old woman who lived in the shack known as the "Long Low Log House." He had a motive for her actions, too, if one were needed. She had tried to buy a field from him and McDonald had refused. He became convinced that it was this old woman who was causing him so much trouble.

He knew that a witch would try to borrow something from her victim so that she could have this person in her power. Now he remembered something that had previously seemed unimportant. The old woman had come to his father's house and asked his sister-in-law to weave her a piece of carpet. His sister-in-law had declined, saying that she would not be able to do any work until the "goings-on" had subsided. It was then that the old woman had said, "Oh, but no trouble will hurt this house as long as you are engaged on my business."

The remark had held no significance for McDonald at the time. But now, in light of his heightened suspicions, he read a sinister undertone in the words. He decided that the old woman was indeed a witch and that it was she who was responsible for all that had been happening to him. He believed that she had put a spell on his household and decided to take action. He would somehow get Troyer to come to the farm, but first he had to provide for his family.

With winter soon approaching, McDonald knew that he and his children could no longer live in the tents. With the help of neighbours, he patched his house as best he could, enough to make it a shelter from the weather. Neighbours' charity fed his family. McDonald was grateful, but humiliated by the need. He continued to brood about the witch and the trouble she had brought on him. The more he brooded, the angrier he got, and the more resolute he became about taking action.

In January 1831, the Reverend McDorman, a Methodist elder, was a guest at Daniel McDonald's house. Reverend McDorman had no reservations about recommending that McDonald seek the help of Troyer, the witch hunter. The Methodist elder seemed familiar with Troyer — he even knew that Troyer had trained one of his daughters to be a clairvoyant. McDorman then offered to take McDonald to Troyer's house — a distance of some 130 kilometres through swamp and thick forest. McDonald accepted the generous offer. He was still fearful of Troyer and of seeking his help, but he was emboldened by the obvious respect with which Reverend McDorman spoke of him.

When the weather cleared, McDonald and the Methodist elder mounted their horses and set off along the narrow trail. They travelled for two days and a night, seldom stopping for rest. On the evening of the second day, they arrived at the Troyers.

For the first time, McDonald realized what an odd sight he and McDorman must have been — tired, cold, and dirty as they were. But the Troyers were unusual, too. Side by side stood the 78-year-old Troyer, with his long white free-flowing hair and long white beard, and his 15-year-old daughter, with her glowing eyes and rapt expression.

When McDonald finished telling them his story, he asked Troyer what lay ahead for him and his family. Troyer turned to his daughter and asked her to tell them McDonald's future.

Miss Troyer was initially unwilling. She was gifted at seeing what others could not, but to do so, she had to gaze into a moonstone that she had found in the fields and polished. With her father's teaching, she had learned to interpret what she saw in the stone's depths, but to do so always frightened her and left her feeling ill.

Her father insisted, so she took the stone from the cupboard and held it in her hands until it warmed from her body's heat. She asked McDonald some questions about the happenings at Baldoon, and then she described his "enemy" to him. There was absolutely no doubt in McDonald's mind now. It was as if the young woman had seen a picture of the old lady at the Long Low Log House. Miss Troyer continued. She told McDonald that as he stood there, his third barn was burning to the ground. Then she and her father told him how to rid himself of the witch.

The young clairvoyant said that the witch shape-changed into the form of an animal in order to persecute him without detection. Could he recall seeing an animal on his farm that did not belong there? Once he identified the animal, she advised McDonald to shoot it with a silver bullet. This was the only way he could rid himself of the witch.

McDonald thought back to his farm. So many of his stock had died that there were few left. But lately he had seen a Canada goose mingle with his domestic flock. When he told this to Miss Troyer, she said, "Yes. The black-headed goose is the one you want."

Troyer intervened, announcing that he would return to Baldoon with McDonald to supervise the exercise. At 78, Troyer was still a crack shot and there was no chance that the goose would escape. Besides, he wanted to make sure that McDonald only injured the goose, not killed it. Troyer wanted the witch to suffer for a very long time.

Early the next day, Troyer and McDonald set out for Baldoon. On the third morning, they started down the hill to the settlement. Even from this distance, they could see the smoke rising from what remained of McDonald's third and last barn. It was just as Miss Troyer had foretold. McDonald dismounted at the house and quickly asked if the wild goose was still with his flock of geese. Then he saw it for himself — black head and two dark feathers on each wing. That evening, with Troyer's help, he fashioned a silver bullet from a spoon and loaded it into his gun.

The next morning dawned bright. McDonald asked his neighbours if they would come and bear witness to what he was about to do. When he had their agreement, he told them his plan. Together, they walked down to the Ecarte River. McDonald focused his gaze so that he saw nothing but the wild goose. He took aim, mindful of Troyer's advice that he only wound and not kill the bird, and then he pulled the trigger. The bird gave a cry and struggled into the taller reeds, dragging an obviously injured left wing behind it. Now came the task of unmasking the witch.

McDonald, Troyer, and the neighbours set off for the Long Low Log House in the damp ravine. Though the sun was high, the mist still clung to the trees and grasses in this dark place. Without knocking, but with some fear, McDonald raised the latch, pushed open the door, and marched into the house, followed by the others. It was as Troyer had foretold on the long ride home. The old woman sat in her chair by the fire, nursing her obviously injured left arm. McDonald was amazed and relieved. Perhaps the bewitching was finally over.

It was said that McDonald suffered no more damage to his property after the unmasking of the witch, but neither did he prosper. The old lady continued to live in the Long Low Log House but was ostracized by the entire community until she died or left — no one could say for certain which, for none went near her house. Troyer returned home and continued hunting witches for another decade.

Chapter 4
Healers

n 1837, a smallpox epidemic swept through Western Canada, decimating the population of the Native prairie tribes. A vaccine programme slowed the onslaught, but it was the magical properties of a lake that cured the Assiniboine. One hundred years later, a physician in the east single-handedly revived the finances of an entire village with his magic fingers, and a stranger in the west brought miraculous healing to the community of Cloverdale, Manitoba. Sometimes it was hard to determine where medicine ended and magic began.

Medicine and Magic
In the spring of 1837, Native peoples of the Cree, Blood, and Blackfoot tribes crossed over the border from Saskatchewan

into North Dakota. They had come to trade as they did each spring, bringing their furs and horses and exchanging them for guns, utensils, and other products made in the east. Every year, they camped on the grasslands near Fort McKenzie, waiting for the longboat laden with supplies to travel up the Missouri River. But this year, they would return home with more than they had bargained for.

They noticed immediately that something was different. Men from the fort rode out to the camps and told them to turn around and go back home, that there was sickness at the fort and that they would all become ill if they came any closer. Alexander Culbertson, commander at Fort McKenzie, was insistent. He warned them that while the longboat carried goods, it also carried something that could wipe out their entire nation. It carried smallpox.

Culbertson knew well the dangers this disease presented. It had filled the churchyards of England with corpses, discriminating against no one, neither pauper nor royalty. Nearly 10 percent of all deaths in England in the 1700s were credited to smallpox. And Culbertson knew that smallpox didn't just ravage people's health, scar their faces, and leave them blind. It made them deaf, crippled their joints, and killed them in astonishing numbers. He dreaded the result of a smallpox epidemic among his trading partners. It was good for neither people nor business.

Seven hundred kilometres to the east, at Fort Union, Montana, a similar event was taking place as Assiniboine and Peigan peoples approached the fort to get supplies for the summer months. When the commander at Fort Union had noted the first sign of sickness, he took the precaution of inoculating his men against the disease. Taking blood from the first smallpox victim, he injected the virus into any who were willing to receive it. Few refused. What the commander didn't understand was that while the inoculation of live virus prevented his men from dying of the disease, it made them carriers of smallpox. So it was that everyone at Fort Union who had not been inoculated became ill with smallpox.

At first, the commander tried to quarantine the area. Like his fellow commander at Fort McKenzie, he sent riders out to the Native camps. The Native people, however, did not understand how the sickness could travel from one person to another. If one man is wounded, they said, the man next to him does not suffer injury. Never before had the Native peoples been exposed to the effects of such a highly contagious disease.

During the following week, more than 1000 men, women, and children of the tribes went to the fort. They traded goods, they took orders for their next trip, and they shared the news of their villages.

Within the month, more than 850 Peigan and Blood died of smallpox. Teepees were filled with the dead and corpses littered the grasslands. Less than 150 of the original 1000 were left to stagger home, if they were able. But smallpox had gone ahead of them, carried by those healthy enough to leave Fort McKenzie and Fort Union before becoming ill. As the weakened Native peoples travelled home, they walked through villages exterminated by the disease. The men of the community had been the first to die, consumed by the illness as they hunted for food. The women and children, starved and overcome by smallpox, became food for the wolves and vultures that were drawn to the camps by the smell of so much death.

William Todd, physician and chief factor at the Swan River Hudson Bay Company District, was unaware of the approaching calamity. On September 20, 1837, when an Assiniboine arrived at Fort Pelly and informed Dr. Todd that a "bad disease had got into the American Fort," and that the gates had been closed and no Natives allowed to enter, Dr. Todd suspected smallpox. There was little else that would cause the fort to close down during the peak of trade. He immediately began a vaccination program for his staff, the Native peoples in his vicinity, and those who travelled to his post. His vaccine was different than the one that had been used at Fort Union. It was derived from cowpox and did not cause those vaccinated to become carriers of the disease.

Dr. Todd was an experienced physician and had seen much illness during his time in Canada. He had joined the Hudson Bay Company in 1816, first as a surgeon at Cumberland House, then at York Factory, Athabasca, and the Red River colonies. Now in his 50s, he was well respected by Natives and HBC traders. More importantly, he returned that respect.

A month later, on October 18, 1837, Dr. Todd was given an explanation for the closing of the fort to the Assiniboine. In his journal, he recorded that an "Indian arrived [who] contradicted the report of any bad disease being at the American Fort." That man's explanation for the exclusion of the Assiniboine was that there had been Blackfoot at the fort. To allow both tribes to stay at the fort together was to court trouble. The explanation sounded reasonable to Dr. Todd and he wondered whether he had been premature with his vaccination program.

Nine days later, on October 27, 1837, another Assiniboine arrived at Fort Pelly. He said that 18 people in his camp had died of smallpox. Dr. Todd was truly alarmed now. Here was confirmation of his worst fear.

The HBC had previously sent the smallpox vaccine to each of their posts in Canada and ordered the traders to dispense it in "the interest of humanity and business." Few of the traders in other HBC posts had followed orders. Dr. Todd, however, did. He expanded his vaccination program, telling those who refused the offer that they would become sick and die. Dr. Todd not only inoculated many men, women, and children, he also took his inoculation program a step further and trained some of the Native men to administer the vaccines to others of their tribe. Dr. Todd initiated the first ever vaccination program amongst the Native peoples of Western Canada.

On October 28, Dr. Todd sent a shipment of vaccine to

William McKay at Beaver Creek. The Assiniboine had travelled through Beaver Creek, and though McKay had made no mention of smallpox at his post, the vaccine would do no harm and might possibly save lives.

Then there was more confusion. On November 6, 1837, William McKay reported from Beaver Creek that there was indeed a disease among the Assiniboine of his area. McKay could not identify the disease, he stated, but he was certain that it was not smallpox.

It was to be another six weeks before smallpox was confirmed as the disease decimating the camps of the Assiniboine. By then it was too late for the recalcitrant HBC traders to vaccinate the people of their areas. The disease had spread north to Carlton House on the North Saskatchewan River. Rumour suggested that the disease was rampant throughout the province of Saskatchewan. More bad news followed. Smallpox was reported as far north and west as Fort Edmonton, in the province of Alberta. More than half of the peoples of the Blackfoot, Blood, Peigan, Circee, and Gros Ventres had died.

The artist George Caitlin, travelling while he did his portraits of the West and its people, wrote in a letter that the Natives "are fast perishing, and will probably, before many years have passed, be an extinct race." Indeed, Dr. Todd was in a desperate struggle against time and disease. If he lost, it would mean the end of the prairie Native peoples.

He expanded his immunization programme, reaching

as many of the Native peoples as he was able. He sent word out to the other HBC posts encouraging them to continue their efforts to bring the disease under control. All the while, he kept detailed journal notes. Dr. Todd was a meticulous physician and he recognized the significance of his vaccination programme. Foregoing sleep, he recorded the names of all those who had been immunized. In a separate list, he recorded the fate of those who had rejected the offer of the vaccine from him or one of the Native people he had trained.

By late winter, the disease had run its course. More than 75 percent of the population of some of the Plains tribes was dead. To Dr. Todd's immense relief and clinical satisfaction, none of the people vaccinated by himself, McKay, or the Native "medics" had died. He credited this fact to the efficacy of the vaccine. The Native peoples felt it might be due to some other ability on Dr. Todd's part. Had he not predicted the death of those who refused the vaccine? In what kind of sorcery or conjuring had he been engaged? Dr. Todd, the man of science, was uncomfortable with the new image of himself as a conjurer, but he was to hear a tale of magical healing that seemed no less credible.

When the Assiniboine were able to travel again and visit the fort, they told Dr. Todd a strange tale. A small number of their tribe had been at Fort Union, but had left as soon as people started to fall ill. They had hoped to race ahead of the illness, to reach home and escape it, but they were already ill. Each day they grew weaker and travelled shorter distances. Travelling east to the Fort Qu'Appelle Valley, trying to outdistance themselves from the disease, they entered a glacier-scooped valley, five kilometres north of present day Watrous, Saskatchewan.

The group, trudging slowly now as they carried two of their tribe, came upon a lake. Its waters were of a curious colour, more of a metallic bronze than a blue. There, on the shore of the lake, they set up a teepee. Two of their people were too weak to continue and were left behind with enough food to last a few days. None of them expected to make it back to their own village.

One of the men, seeking relief from his fever, crawled to the edge of the lake where the waves lapped onto the shore. He scooped water into his mouth, drinking deeply, but it was salty and he spat it out. Instead, he inched his way deeper into the water. So feverish was he that he gave no thought to drowning. In fact, he seemed to be floating on the surface of the water, as if the water held him up. He lay there the rest of that day and all through the night.

In the morning, he woke as if from a deep sleep and had the strength to crawl to the teepee and drag and coax his friend to the water. He immersed himself in the water, and gently drew his friend in beside him. As before, he floated, as did his friend. That afternoon, he felt strong enough to crawl to the teepee and bring back food and water for the two of them. Within a few days, both men had recovered from the smallpox and were able to catch up to their original group, though they had been at the lake almost a week.

Dr. Todd was unsure whether to believe the story or not, but it was apparent that the Native peoples recognized and spoke openly of the healing properties of the lake. They called it Little Manitou Lake, the Lake of the Healing Waters, or the Lake of Good Spirit. With time, homesteaders travelled to fill barrels with water from the lake, for it was rumoured that cuts and scratches healed almost instantly after being immersed in its waters. Travelling medicine men learned of its curative power and sold the water as a hair tonic, a cure for skin conditions, rheumatism, and, presumably, smallpox.

In the 1920s and 1930s, Little Manitou Lake was "redis-covered" and became a popular tourist attraction. People came for the mineral waters and for the healing that it was said to effect. While only 200 people lived on its shores in the winter, the population in summer would rise to 15,000. Today the area is home to a spa and Camp Easter Seal — a summer camp for handicapped children. Chemical analysis of the water has shown that it contains natural therapeutic proper-ties found in only two other locations in the world — Karlovy Vary in the Czechoslovakian Republic and the Dead Sea in Israel. Both areas are well-known healing centres.

Dr. Mahlon Locke: The Toe-Twister of Williamsburg

In July of 1932, it was virtually impossible to drive into the village of Williamsburg, Ontario. It wasn't that the roads were poor, but rather that the streets were clogged with people.

People filled the roads; they filled the sidewalks and the parks. There were people in wheelchairs. There were people being carried on stretchers, and there were children and adults on crutches. They were all there to receive treatment from Dr. Mahlon Locke, known variously as the "Toe-Twister of Williamsburg" and the "Wizard of Williamsburg."

At a time when the rest of the country was suffering from the worst economic depression in Canadian history, Williamsburg was thriving. The curious thing was that the growth of the town was due to the wizard's skill with feet.

This unusual vocation had come to Dr. Locke through a circuitous route. His father had died when Dr. Locke was only eight, and the boy had then taken on many of the responsibilities of the family farm. By the time he was in high school, the demands of farming meant that he had missed so much school he was not allowed to graduate. Undeterred, he invested his considerable creativity into making the farm a success.

His mother invested her skills and energy into getting her son back in school. Dr. Locke returned to classes after an absence of several years. Within a month he had completed and passed the requirements for his high school matriculation. Next, he enrolled at Queen's University. Four years later he had graduated from its medical school and gone into practice with his new stepfather, Dr. G.W. Collison. Dr. Locke was soon bored and discouraged. After six months of exhausting work as a country doctor, he had only $15 in savings to show for his effort. He looked for a new challenge.

In 1906, Dr. Locke accepted a position as company doctor with Algoma Steel in Sault Ste. Marie. He earned the then-princely sum of $100 per month. Still, he felt under-challenged and after only a year at Algoma, he went to Scotland to study at the Royal Infirmary in Edinburgh. It was there that Dr. Locke developed his interest and specialization in orthopedics. These skills and techniques would end up supporting, quite literally, an entire community.

When Dr. Locke returned from Scotland, he purchased the practice of a retiring country doctor. He delivered babies, vaccinated children, and sat by dying patients. When his sled tipped on the way home from a call, he simply wrapped himself up in his bearskin robe and slept at the side of the path. All the time, his fascination with the mechanics of the skeleton grew. He had treated many broken bones at Algoma — steel mills had their share of industrial accidents. Now he was in farming country, and the parade of broken bones, dislocated joints, and amputated limbs continued. There were also patients with arthritis.

It was with these patients that Dr. Locke honed in on what was to become a world famous gift of healing — a skill that brought patients from as far away as South America, Holland, England, and Norway to the little Canadian village of Williamsburg.

Dr. Locke's theory was uncomplicated. He noted that too many of his patients suffered from both crippling

arthritis and flat feet for there not to be a connection. He reasoned that fallen arches "press onto the main nerves leading
into the foot, irritating it. This constricts the arteries, and the
blood, moving sluggishly, becomes full of impurities, par-
ticularly uric acid which attacks the places of least resistance
(i.e., the joints)." His plan was simple: force the arch back,
thereby relieving the pressure on the nerve and increasing
the circulation of blood. That way, he said, the blood would
carry impurities to the liver and kidneys where they could be
properly expelled from the body.

His first attempt brought him instant recognition. Peter
Beckstead was a local blacksmith. Everybody in Williamsburg
knew Beckstead, and they knew that he was crippled with
rheumatism, knew that it wouldn't be long before the pain
got so bad that Beckstead would have to stop shoeing horses.
As it was, he had already given up some of his clients because
he was unable to shoe the younger, more restless animals.
Beckstead came to see Dr. Locke, to see if the doctor had
anything that would relieve the pain.

After a few weeks, people noticed that Beckstead walked
easier, that he didn't seem bent over in pain all the time. He
told them Dr. Locke was fixing him up. After a few more
weeks, Beckstead was able to take back those clients with
more difficult horses. What was this miracle treatment of
Dr. Locke's?

The doctor's wizardry was simply a combination of
massages and manipulations that returned the arch of the

foot to its proper alignment. In order to keep it there, he designed a special shoe with an arch support, or "cookie," as he called it. Dr. Locke was a practical man. He reasoned that the foot carried a heavy load all day long, day after day, year after year. He extrapolated that thought to the idea of a building whose foundation had caved in or collapsed. Surely, he reasoned, the building would have to collapse or be severely compromised in that instance. Why would not the same theory apply to the feet? Beckstead was living, walking proof that his theory worked.

Beckstead was also a loquacious man. As he shod people's horses or fabricated staves for their apple barrels, he talked of the doctor's magic fingers. Six months earlier he had been on the verge of ruin. Now he was busier than ever. Word spread to neighbouring New York State. From Lockport came Father Kelly, a priest so crippled with arthritis that he had difficulty alighting from his carriage at Dr. Locke's house. Again, within six months, Dr. Locke had wrought a miraculous-seeming cure. The priest, so crippled before, was now able to walk to his parishioners' homes. A newspaper article was written, and then another. Soon hundreds of patients arrived, eager to benefit from Dr. Locke's magic hands. Williamsburg was about to change from a sleepy village to a bustling town.

Many of his patients were from close by. But one, Jock MacDonald, travelled all the way from Unity, Saskatchewan. Travelled was perhaps a misnomer. Jock was transported from Unity on a mattress in the baggage car of a train. Only 16 years old, he was virtually paralysed by arthritis and debilitating pain. He weighed only 91 pounds when Dr. Locke first met him. His left arm was frozen, his fingers deformed and curled, and one of his legs was contracted and locked at the hip.

Dr. Locke set to work. As he massaged the young boy's arches, Jock experienced pins and needles in his feet. Then his feet began to burn and throb. After a week of treatment several times a day, Jock became violently ill with vomiting and diarrhea. Jock's father, who had travelled with his son, was concerned and wondered whether they should stop, or slow down treatment. Not at all, said Dr. Locke. This is exactly what we want. He believed that the young man's body was finally getting rid of the toxins in his system, toxins that had built up over the years of his illness and immobility.

Over a period of months, Jock gradually regained the use of his legs. He walked with crutches at first, but after two years could walk with the aid of a cane. By the end of the third year of treatment, Jock was able to ride a bicycle. The treatment was life-changing for Jock and his father. With the obvious improvements to his son's health brought about by Dr. Locke, Mr. MacDonald was keen to stay in the Williamsburg area. He was a journalist by trade, and so he did the logical thing. He started a newsletter, a newsletter that had only one topic — the miracle cures of Dr. Locke.

Word got out to more and more people. Then Mr.

MacDonald wrote a book about Dr. Locke and the doctor's fame became international. The road to Williamsburg now had to be hard-surfaced; so many people were travelling on the dirt road that it was unnavigable in the spring thaw as hundreds of cars headed to Williamsburg. New travel routes had to be devised — the roads couldn't handle the volume.

So many Americans were seeking the assistance of Dr. Locke that the ferry company increased the number of runs for its Waddington, New York to Morrisburg, Ontario route. Then they increased them again, and again, until finally they had quadrupled the number of crossings in a day. That increase still wasn't sufficient to transport the people who sought the doctor's treatments. The company added a second ferry to the crossing. Eventually, there was a ferry running every 15 minutes from early morning to late at night.

Williamsburg was a boomtown. Two hotels were built to house the patients, but there was still need for more accommodations. Someone had the idea of using a boat as a floating hotel. Within a very short time, the liner the *Rapids Queen* was anchored at Morrisburg. That increased the number of available "staterooms" by 65. The need for accommodations continued to increase. Farmers, who a year earlier were feeling the pinch of the Depression, rented out every conceivable room in their farmhouses, while their children slept in the barns with the animals. Cottages were built, old implement sheds renovated, and chicken coops cleaned and scoured with lye.

The community was under siege. Wells ran dry and stores were emptied of goods. Sewage disposal became a problem and garbage accumulated. Never had so small a town had to deal with so many people for so long. And still more came. They came by car and limousine, and they came by private plane and yacht. Some patients hitchhiked. One rode the entire way from California in the back of an ancient pick-up. Mackenzie King was one of Dr. Locke's patients, as were Lady Eaton and Mrs. F.D. Roosevelt. As the fame of his patients became known, the doctor's appeal increased. By 1931, he was seeing an unbelievable 1000 patients a day.

Dr. Locke could probably have built himself a comfortable clinic, but he was a man who enjoyed the outdoors and he had no intention of being confined in a building hour after hour. He saw his patients on the west lawn of his property. To do so efficiently, he devised a spoke wheel. In the centre of his lawn, he built a wooden platform on which he placed his low, swivel doctor's chair. From that central hub there radiated 14 "spokes," each of them divided by iron pipes. Each of the spokes was a runway down which the lines of people would travel. Two of the runways were reserved for stretchers and wheelchairs. Some people stood the entire time; some carried footstools or campstools. Others simply brought a cushion and leaned against the pipes. Slowly, the people made their way to the centre of the hub, where a wooden treatment chair was placed at the end of each runway. The patient would sit in the chair and wait for Dr. Locke to make his way around the hub, swivelling his chair as he turned from one patient to another. On occasion, the doctor would stand up and let his chair unwind. Then he would sit down again and begin the slow wind of the chair.

Each morning, Dr. Locke would exit his house to the sound of a cheer from the gathered people. He would make his way to the centre and begin with the first patient, accepting a dollar and only a dollar from each person. That dollar would cover the day's treatment, whether it was only one treatment or two. He would grasp a foot and "press up the arch with one quick movement of the thumb while he twisted the toes down and out with the other hand." He would release the foot, accept his dollar payment, and swivel his chair to face the next patient, and the next. He took no reservations and treated everybody on a first come first served basis. Every now and then he would get up and go into the house, where he emptied the dollar bills that bulged the pockets of his jacket and trousers. At the end of the day, he would go into his home and reportedly paint his thumbs with iodine.

His practice grew. An East Indian merchant prince travelled from Bombay with his private physician, who was intent on learning Dr. Locke's secret. Trains made unscheduled stops to let patients get on and off and the number of restaurants in Williamsburg rose from 3 to an incredible 23. With the fame came questions. There were questions about his qualifications, his treatment, and his ethics. Was it right that he diagnosed foot ailments and then sold shoes to these people — shoes that were relatively expensive?

Dr. Locke passed the test with flying colours. He was not only licensed to practice medicine in Canada, but was licensed to practice in Scotland. His treatment seemed to work. As far as the possible conflict of interest with the shoe factory, he solved that dilemma by selling the patent to a Perth, Ontario company. Regardless, an article in the November 1932 Journal of the *American Medical Association* labeled Dr. Locke a quack — a "faith-healer who practices the laying on of hands." Part of the problem was that other practitioners had tried to practice his methods, but were unable to create the same results. The controversy only heightened Dr. Locke's fame.

At the peak of his career in 1937, he was treating 2700 people, twice daily. On a regular day he worked from eight in the morning, until eleven at night. On some days, wakened by the crowds that began lining up at one in the morning, he would exit the house at five a.m., sit quietly in his chair, and reach for the first foot. Dr. Locke maintained the incredible pace for ten years. In the winter, he moved his clinic into a converted and heated drive shed.

The pace began to wear on him. He developed diabetes and recurrent pneumonia. Still the people came, intruding on him in his sickbed, if he didn't come outside. In 1941, when Dr. Locke was 61 years of age, he was still seeing 500 to 600 patients a day. Only death would free him from their demands.

Healers

On February 7, 1942, Dr. Locke suffered a stroke after a car accident. He never regained consciousness and died that evening. His friend, Lewis Schell, blamed his death on his fame. That's what killed him, he said. "He had plenty to do right around here without all those people."

John Love: Miracle Worker
In September 1934, farmer Archie Fitch of Oak Hammock, Manitoba, watched a slightly built and unimpressive man walk up to his farmhouse door. The man had a woman and child with him and they looked cold and miserable. Fitch guessed that the man was seeking shelter from the rain for himself and his family. When Fitch opened the door, the stranger's first words to him were, "I knew you were sick." So began the 42-day meteoric rise and fall of the healer John Love.

Fitch had indeed been ill. He had sought some relief by going to doctors in Winnipeg, but they had been unable to diagnose his illness or suggest a treatment for his chronic pain. When John Love told Fitch that his illness and suffering were over, Fitch was sceptical. Love challenged Fitch to try and do something physical that he had previously been unable to do. Fitch did, and was amazed. He lifted a stack of wood — something that had been beyond his strength a week ago.

The farmer told his friends of the miracle that had occurred. Neighbours began to call — to bring their arthritic limbs, their rheumatic hearts, their aching backs, and their crippled legs. Some immediately claimed they felt better, that the doctor had cured them. Word spread farther afield, carried by delivery truck and migrant workers. Farm boys told their friends, who told their friends, so that on Saturday, October 13, 1934, when reporter John Sweeney of the *Winnipeg Free Press* showed up to cover the story, he had a difficult time finding a place to park his car.

Even getting to the farm had been a challenge. The Parkdale Highway was rutted, and the thousands of wheels that had traversed that road since the news of the healing had been broadcast had churned up the crossroad at the turnoff to the Fitch place. Sweeney left his car some distance from the house — he could get no closer because of all the cars parked on the road allowance. Every conceivable space in the farmyard had a car on it.

Sweeney mingled with the 100-plus people. He saw men and women — the elderly and the very young. He counted cripples, the blind, and the retarded. No one seemed in a hurry. They spoke quietly amongst themselves, waiting in line for an invitation to enter the farmhouse door.

Every few minutes, Mrs. Love would come to the door and walk amongst the people. Seemingly at random, she would choose someone to follow her into the house. On occasion, Mrs. Fitch would mingle with the people, inviting someone to follow her. Some people never got in to see Love, though they waited 12 hours or more. Others were admitted immediately upon arrival.

The reporter was intrigued. He heard from one person that on Saturday, October 6, more than 150 people had been admitted into the doctor's presence. Sweeney approached the house and asked if he could speak with Love. But Love, through his wife, informed Sweeney that he "would neither talk to a newspaperman, nor permit one to watch him."

Sweeney asked Mrs. Love to describe what her husband did. "Is it faith healing?" he inquired.

Mrs. Love responded that her husband "was neither a faith healer nor a divine healer, and that he resented both terms when applied to him." Sweeney persisted, but Mrs. Love explained that her husband fit no ordinary category. She and her husband claimed no alliance with any religious denomination; she said they made their own interpretation of the Bible.

More surprisingly, Love's wife claimed that while the healing might be important, it was not her husband's prime focus. She claimed that her husband's "ability to perform cures is a physical manifestation of a spiritual power which directs him along a road, where he is the only traveler." Her husband was "ascending from a low plane of enlightenment to a higher one," she said.

"What is this guiding spiritual force?" asked Sweeney.

"The word of God," answered Mrs. Love.

Love appeared to gain no financial reward. He refused payment, though he did accept food and clothing for his family and presumably the Fitches, who by this time had been hosting the trio of Loves for more than a month.

Again, Sweeney mingled with the crowd. He was learning little from Mrs. Love, had been refused admission to the house, and did not yet have much of a story. Among the crowd he found a few leads. Three people claimed that they had regained their sight, two deaf-mutes had begun to hear and speak, and most incredibly, Love appeared to have cured a woman who had not even been on the Fitch farm, but had remained at home in Winnipeg.

Sweeney was enraptured by this last story. It appeared that an elderly woman had lost her speech and her movement as the result of a devastating stroke. Her son had come out to see Love to ask him whether he should bring his mother to the farm. It would be a very difficult trip for her, he'd said, and he didn't want to put her through it if Love was unable to see her. He feared she might even be made worse by the ordeal.

"Not necessary," said Love. He followed that comment with the statement that if the young man were to return home, he would find his mother on the road to recovery. On returning home, the man found that his mother had indeed regained her speech. Five days later she was walking.

Love's power seemed to be increasing. While he saw some patients, he often sent messages to others in the crowd through these patients, declaring that they should return home, that they would be cured the next day. There were even some, Sweeney was told, who had long been victims of mental illness, who had their minds "righted" by a single visit.

Sweeney still had not been able to "see" the treatment. He waited for darkness and the thinning of the crowd around the house. A lamp went on in the living room where Love was seated. The reporter watched him intently. Sweeney described Love in that day's article, "Miraculous Cures are Credited to Mystery Man on Manitoba Farm," as about 5 feet, 10 inches in height and approximately 130 pounds in weight. He looked to be about 45 to 50, his hair receded from his forehead and was dark and thick and streaked with grey. Most remarkable were his eyes. They "flashed brilliantly and seemed the colour of a deep, red ruby," read the *Winnipeg Free Press* story.

Sweeney observed the man's actions. Love would approach his patients and sometimes touch them briefly. On a few occasions he would massage the area identified as troublesome. "Where are you from?" he would ask. "How long have you been like this?" He would then tell them that they could leave, that they were cured. Sweeney tried to talk with the people as they exited the house, but they were all silent as they walked to their cars and drove away.

On Tuesday, another article appeared in the *Winnipeg Free Press*. Activity on the farm had continued over the weekend with one notable exception. Visitors to the farm on the Sunday arrived to find that Love had decamped, moving with his wife and daughter to more spacious accommodations at the Cloverdale farm of Mrs. J.R. Sutherland. The people, intent on their cure, simply continued on there, following directions provided by Mrs. Fitch. More than 100 cars were said to travel the road between the two farms that day.

On Wednesday, Sweeney had another article in the paper. He had been out to the farm on the Monday and had counted an astonishing 63 cars parked in the Sutherland yard. By noon, there were 78, each of them bearing four or more passengers. Again the method of admission seemed random. People would be admitted from the line as others exited the house. Occasionally Mrs. Love would approach one of the cars and invite a passenger to accompany her into the house and presence of "Doctor" Love. There was one difference, however.

Love had established visiting hours. He saw people from 10 to 12 in the morning and 2 to 5 in the afternoon. At five o'clock, people were told that the "doctor" would see no more that day. Though some might have been waiting in line since eight in the morning, they left unseen with scarcely a protest.

Sweeney again attempted to interview Love. Again he was deterred, but Mrs. Love did ask to speak with him. She had a complaint. In Sweeney's first article, printed on the 13th, he had reported that Love "was guided by the word of God." Not so, said Mrs. Love. "He is the word of God."

Through further questioning, Sweeney was able to learn that Love would remain in the area until "directed elsewhere."

Curiously, Mrs. Love added that her husband had no intention of continuing his healing work indefinitely. He had other areas of his work that needed attention, she said. Sweeney asked whether they felt bad for the people who had travelled many miles to see them without gaining admittance to Love. She replied that they felt no responsibility, for they had not asked them to come.

Sweeney set out to gather some proof of Love's fraud or miracle work. He himself was not sure which it was. He spoke with a young girl, a victim of infantile paralysis. He had heard through the murmuring of the crowd that she had first attended the "doctor" on crutches, but that after several treatments, she needed only a cane. Sweeney had set out to find her.

The story was inconclusive. She stated that in fact she had never needed crutches, but had always walked with a cane. After her third treatment, Love had encouraged her to walk without it. She had tried to do so, but had been unable to support herself. Love is a fraud, thought Sweeney. However, the girl added, she did feel not only better, but also seemed to have gained some strength in her back. Sweeney was back where he started.

The next story he heard was also inconclusive He spoke with a 60-year-old severe arthritic who had been unable to open or close his hands and had needed to use a cane to walk. Love had taken this man's hands, pried them open, massaged them, and opened and closed them several times.

After Love's "healing," the man could perform the previously impossible task himself, but he still needed his crutches.

It was at this juncture that Love took on another persona. He had been told of a young woman, a single mother, who had a stomach tumour. She required surgery, but had neither the money nor the circumstances that would allow her to have it, having no one to care for her children if she were to enter hospital. A neighbour had come to Love to advocate on her behalf. Would Love see her?

"No need," said Love. "She will be cured." The patient said later that she went to bed that night full of worry for her future and the future of her children. Despite her worries, she dreamed. In that dream, angels appeared at her bedside accompanied by a man who was unknown to her. She said that the man directed the angels to remove the tumour from her body, and they did so.

In the morning, the woman woke. She no longer felt any pain. She got up and cared for her children — again without the constant pain of the last weeks. Several days later, she went to her door in response to a knock. To her amazement, the man in her dream was standing on the doorstep. It was John Love.

On Thursday, October 18, a different reporter, Burt Gresham, went out to the farm. Mrs. Love was more talkative with Gresham than she had been with Sweeney. She had three facts to impart. First, she said her husband was "the Word," but not, she exclaimed angrily, "the Word of God," as

Sweeney had reported. The second thing she wanted clear up was that the Day of Judgment had come, and the third, that she was Irish. This last declaration made little sense to Gresham, but it was to prove important.

Again, she denied the reporter access to her husband, stating that Love did not need him or anybody else to complete his plans. Her husband had found enlightenment and to him all things were possible. He could, she said, choose to heal anyone. His choice as to whom he helped seemed to be based on his assessment of "where they stood in relation to the law." Success in healing was not the goal, she said.

Things then took another strange twist. Mrs. Love claimed that because of her husband's enlightenment, she had been given "complete protection against all adversity."

"Does that protection extend to your daughter as well?" asked Gresham. Mrs. Love responded that, "Eternal punishment would befall anyone who harmed their child." Then she threatened the members of the press who were present, stating that, "Terrible and mysterious consequences would fall on any who criticized or made derogatory comments about the couple."

"Mr. Love," she said, "is the Word. He is of a vastly higher plane than human beings." The reporters asked permission to photograph the family. That was denied. They asked if the family possessed a photograph that they could use and return. There never had been a photo, was the reply. Most curiously, Mrs. Love announced, "I am Irish myself, you know."

There it was again, that seemingly inconsequential statement that was obviously of some significance to Mrs. Love.

That last strange comment, so casually spoken yet so clearly important to her, would eventually enable Sweeney to trace the origins of the family. But not yet. The frenzy surrounding the Loves' work continued.

On Friday, October 19, reporter Sweeney was back on the beat. Two hundred automobiles converged on the farm that day, full of people seeking cures. One of the cars had travelled all the way from Ontario. Telegrams, telephone calls, and letters poured into the office of the *Winnipeg Free Press* seeking confirmation or denial of "Dr." Love's abilities as a healer. Stories of miraculous cures were heard, but they were all second, third, or fourth hand. There were now more people who claimed that they were no better after treatment.

Then came a break in the story. Someone recognized that the tale of John Love of Cloverdale bore a striking similarity to the story of a John Love who been in Ottawa the previous year. People who had spoken with Mrs. Love declared that she did indeed seem to have an unusual interest in any news from eastern Ontario. But the Loves remained silent on the subject.

Just when it appeared that John Love might be an ordinary human being, with no known history or talent for healing, more than a dozen patients came forward to attest to his ability as a healer. A Mr. W. Stevenson of Selkirk, Manitoba, had a curious tale. He had approached Love about the loss of his sight seven years ago after drinking "canned heat," a kind of methyl alcohol used in cook stoves. He said that Love had asked him a few questions, "put his fingers in my ears for a minute, then told me to go home, that I would be alright and that my hearing would be better too."

The odd thing was that Stevenson had never told Love that he was hard of hearing — that he had "noise like steam engines in my ears all the time" after a tree had fallen on his head.

Stevenson said, and proved to reporter Sweeney, that he could now read licence plates at a 30-foot distance. Not only that, but he could now carry on a conversation in a normal voice and the hissing noise in his ears had ceased. Six other remarkable stories of rheumatism cured, stomach ailments vanquished, pain vanished, strength regained, and eyesight restored were told. Now, there was also a claim that Love could divine the future. He had apparently told someone that he would receive an important phone call, and, lo and behold, the phone had rung.

Then things took a downward turn for the Loves. The Monday morning edition of the *Winnipeg Tribune* reported that on Friday, October 19, John Love had refused to see any of the estimated 200 to 250 people who had lined up to seek his assistance, despite the chill and damp of the day. Within the crowd were four blind men who had come all the way from Winnipeg. They had been brought to the farm the day before, but when they were unable to gain access to Love, they had asked to be seen the next day. Love had apparently agreed to see them if they returned in the morning, and so they did, buoyed with hope. However, when they arrived on that Friday as they had been directed, Love turned them away.

They reminded him that he had promised. Still he refused. They told Love of the huge expense that they had gone to to travel there, not once but twice. Love was firm. He directed their driver to return the four men to Winnipeg. On hearing this, the crowd became angry. They spoke out against John Love until his wife came out and, standing on the running board of a car, beseeched them to not lose faith in her husband's healing powers, that if they remained steadfast, they would be cured. Social pressure, however, would eventually deter people from visiting Love.

On Tuesday, October 23, the *Winnipeg Free Press* quoted a report authored by Louis S. Reed, PhD on the subject of religious healing. It credited that healing of a hysterical-type illness was possible. By Friday, readers were shocked out of their seats by an article written by Dr. Henry C. Hall, a Winnipeg physiotherapist. His article started off in a factual way, pointing out that miracle healing could not repair destruction of tissue. By the middle of the first paragraph, Dr. Hall launched into a full frontal attack on not only John Love, but also the people who had sought his assistance.

"Miracle healers," he wrote, "are numbered in direct proportion to the illiteracy of the masses." He continued,

"A very ignorant people will, by virtue of their ignorance, incline towards belief ... which boasts of innumerable miracles." Winnipeggers were stunned. Hall had declared these hundreds of hopeful people illiterate and ignorant. The numbers of cars to the farm dramatically decreased.

On Saturday, the *Winnipeg Free Press* published their last article on the Loves. In it, Mr. John McChesney of Margo, Saskatchewan, stated that he had met the Loves at the time of the birth of their daughter. In a letter to the paper, he wrote that he had no doubt that the couple he had met were the same couple that had been enjoying the hospitality of the people of Cloverdale. McChesney wrote that the Mrs. Love he had met was close to her confinement, and that he had advised her to stay in town until the baby was born. He stated that the family had seemed unconcerned, that they had said they were on a journey across Canada and that someone was looking out for them. Three days later, 250 kilometres to the west, the woman had delivered a baby girl at Quill Lake, Saskatchewan.

The townspeople of Quill Lake had offered their hospitality to the family. It was December and they had encouraged the family to stay until spring. The Loves had declined the offer and had taken to the road three days later, taking turns carrying the infant.

The people of Quill Lake said that there was something curious about the lady. She had repeatedly told people that she was Irish. It seemed very important to her that people knew this about her. This statement alone would verify that they were one and the same family, for hadn't Mrs. Love made that same curious comment in Cloverdale?

There seemed to be no easy answer as to whether John Love was a true healer, or simply a man in need of shelter for his wife and daughter. There was no record of John Love having performed any healings in Margo or Quill Lake, but there had been a curious incident that took place during their time in Margo. One of the farmers was trying to locate water on his property. A 33-metre well had been drilled, but had yielded poor results and the man was not eager to go to the same expense and effort unless he was guaranteed some better results. He had casually asked Love where the water might be.

Love had said nothing. He'd lowered his head onto his hand and remained still. He'd then raised his head, gazed out the window, and said with great certainty, "Seventy yards to the northwest of your farmyard there is a straw stack. A little to the east of the straw and beside a heap of stones, there is a little hollow. Dig there and you will get more water than you want."

Unfortunately, the man had not yet dug on the site and there was no way of verifying whether Love's prediction had been right. As in Cloverdale, there was reason to believe that John Love was a man of talents, a healer of the sick, a finder of water. But before any conclusive proof could be found as to whether he was a healer or a fraud, the Loves moved on, walking side by side, carrying their daughter and fading into obscurity.

Chapter 5
Clairvoyants

he ability to see into the future or the past is neither uncommon nor new. Canadian history records two unique applications of this ability. In one case, clairvoyance was used to solve a recent murder. In the other, to shed light on mysteries that were thousands of years old.

Uncanny Detection: The Detective and the Telepathist
On the evening of July 9, 1928, Vernon Booher reportedly entered the kitchen of his parents' farmhouse near Manville, Alberta. He expected to find his mother preparing a snack for his father or doing one of the countless other chores that kept her busy from early morning until late at night. Instead, he found her lying in a pool of blood on the kitchen floor.

Clairvoyants

Vernon had been a farmer long enough to recognize that she was dead.

Vernon then called out for his older brother Fred. When there was no answer, he went down the hall to his brother's bedroom. There he found Fred, but he too was dead, sprawled on his back on the floor, blood a brilliant backdrop on the wall and floor. Vernon panicked and ran to the bunkhouse to get Gabriel Cromby, one of the farm hands. It was as if Vernon were in a repetitive nightmare, for Gabriel too was dead. Vernon didn't look for the other hired man. Instead, he ran to his neighbour's house to call for a doctor. He knew that everyone at his farm was dead, but he didn't know who else to call.

His neighbours called the police and together with Vernon, awaited their arrival. Vernon told his story over and over again, never changing a detail, his voice a monotone.

While they waited in the cozy kitchen, Henry Booher, Vernon's father, returned from his work in the fields and entered his own house. He, like his son before him, went into the kitchen and bedroom before anyone could warn him of the sights he would see.

Constable Fred Olsen of the Alberta Provincial Police was the first of many policemen to arrive at the farm. He found Henry Booher deep in shock, unable to comprehend the immensity of the tragedy, unable to identify anyone who would have conducted such a slaughter, who would wish this much anguish on his family. It was true that they were successful farmers, but they lived simply, treated others with respect, and were considered to be people of high moral character.

Suspicion fell on the other farm hand — William Rosyk. Why was he not there? Surely he would have heard the commotion in the yard, and later heard the excited voices of the policemen. He wasn't in the bunkhouse. They had already determined that when they viewed Cromby's body. Vernon went with the police to search the barns and outbuildings. There they found Rosyk, and like the others he was dead, shot at close range.

The police arranged for the four bodies to be transported to the hospital for autopsies. Then they began a search of the house and barns for the murder weapon. A search of the grounds and fields would have to wait for daylight. It was soon evident that each of the four — Eunice Booher, her son Frank, and the two hired hands William Rosyk and Gabriel Cromby, had all been shot at close range with a .303 rifle. What puzzled the police though, apart from the lack of an apparent motive, was that the first three victims appeared to have been killed within minutes of each other, while Cromby hadn't been shot until after 8 p.m.— an estimated 90 minutes later. Authorities were certain of this because Vernon said that he had heard the shot while he was working with the livestock. He guessed the time was 8 p.m., and he had thought nothing of the sound of gunfire, for Manville was a hunting area.

Clairvoyants

The next morning, the police returned to the Booher farm. Again they searched the outbuildings and the house. They walked to the well, took the cover off, and sent a man down to search the bottom for the rifle. They also dug through the feed storage bins. They found no weapon. They walked the fence line around the house, but they knew it would be virtually impossible to search the farmland. There was just too much land. The police were stalled in their investigation.

They had four bodies — all shot at close range. Three of them had been shot at around 6:30 p.m. The other at 8 p.m. They had no apparent motive. Although the Boohers were well off, there was no evidence of theft. Unless one could believe that someone had ridden or driven to the farm, exited his car, entered the house and shot two people, gone to the bunkhouse and shot a third, and then bizarrely returned 90 minutes later and shot the fourth person, one had to look at who had opportunity.

That left Henry Booher — husband, father, and employer of the victims — or his son Vernon. No one on the force thought that it was Henry. His shock had been too real, too impossible to pretend. That left 21-year-old Vernon — Vernon, who had found the bodies, Vernon who had supplied the time frame for the fourth shooting. Could Vernon have cold-bloodedly murdered four people? Unlikely, police thought.

They then considered a neighbour — Charles Stevenson. His rifle, a .303, was missing, but he hadn't reported it stolen until the police had asked to see it. He had also admitted to visiting the Boohers on the night of the murder to "look at a farming catalogue," he had told authorities. The police still had no murder weapon and no motive. What they did have was an inquest with a date that was fast approaching.

The three police officers involved — Constable Fred Olsen and Detective Frank Lesley of the Alberta Provincial Police, and Manville town Constable George Milligan — decided that this investigation called for some creative measures. Frankly, they were desperate for a break in the case. Constable Olsen had been a RCMP officer before and still had contacts with police in Vancouver. He knew that Vancouver police had recently used the services of a "mind reader," a Dr. Otto Maximilian Langsner, to solve a jewel robbery. Constable Olsen looked into Dr. Langsner's background. The man had been a student of Freud, specializing in the area of mind control and telepathy. He had then gone on to India to obtain a PhD from the University of Calcutta. He seemed legitimate. Dr. Langsner had conducted investigations for the Shah of Persia (now Iran), the King of Egypt, and the British government. More recently, he had come to Canada to do research with the Inuit and Native peoples. It was while he was in Vancouver that he had assisted the police there by telling them where stolen jewels could be found. Would he come to Manville to assist them with their investigation?

Dr. Langsner agreed and arrived in Manville just as the inquest was to start. He sat in the courtroom, at the press table. He said nothing, asked no questions, and spoke to no one. At the recess, he told Constable Olsen, "I can tell you the name of the killer. It is Vernon Booher."

Constable Olsen accepted this. Certainly the police had had their suspicions, but what they really needed was the murder weapon. They still had no apparent motive. Dr. Langsner said that he could help them with the location of the murder weapon. He said that the gun was hidden in a clump of prairie grass behind the house. Constable Olsen thought that unlikely — police had searched the barn and the fields, and they had even gone into the well. The next day, he and Dr. Langsner accompanied several police officers to the farm.

Dr. Langsner got out of the car and went around to the back of the farmhouse. He walked like a water diviner — except that he had no divining rod. Back and forth he paced, listening with his entire body to signals from the ground. For 20 minutes he walked, stopped, changed direction, and walked on again. He then turned to the policemen who watched him and asked one of them to take 10 paces forward. A constable stepped forward. He took another step, and then another. On the ninth step he stumbled over the .303 hidden in the thick grass. Dr. Langsner told him not to waste his time looking for prints — Vernon had wiped the gun clean.

The police now had the murder weapon, but they still had nothing tying Vernon to the murder. Dr. Langsner suggested that they place Vernon in "protective custody." They did so, telling Vernon that he might be in danger from the killer or killers.

Dr. Langsner entered the cell block and seated himself on a chair outside, but facing Vernon's cell. Vernon recognized him from the inquest. He had seen him at the press table, but he didn't know who he was. He certainly didn't look like anyone from the local papers. Dr. Langsner was a petite man, in the strangest narrow-fitting black suit that Vernon had ever seen. The doctor had untidy white hair flopping on the collar of his shirt. Perhaps Vernon thought the doctor was a reporter who had come to interview him. Dr. Langsner, however, asked no questions. He simply sat in his chair.

Vernon tried to talk to the stranger. He asked him questions, but got no answers. He spoke angrily to him, but still Dr. Langsner ignored him. After 4 hours and 40 minutes, Dr. Langsner stood up, said goodbye to Vernon, and left the cell block to report to Constable Olsen and the others.

He told them that Vernon had hated his mother — that he had gone into the house with the intention of killing her, and had done so by shooting her in the back of the neck. Vernon had thought the house was empty of everyone else, but when the gun had gone off, he'd heard a noise in Fred's room, and realized that his brother was in the house, not in the fields as he had expected. Quickly he had rushed to his brother's bedroom and, as Fred looked at him in amazement, jaw hanging open, Vernon had shot him through the mouth.

Running out of the house, he'd seen Rosyk the farm hand approaching. He had then forced the hand back to the bunkhouse and killed him. Dr. Langsner didn't say what Vernon had done during the next 90 minutes, only that Vernon had been afraid that Cromby might have seen him and had decided to kill him, too.

Constable Olsen felt the story was entirely believable, but he still lacked any sort of proof. The gun, after all, belonged to Charles Stevenson, not Vernon, and the police had nothing to connect Vernon with the weapon. But Dr. Langsner had the answer for that, too.

He told them to find a "little woman with small eyes and a long jaw, who wore a poke bonnet." Dr. Langsner said that this woman had seen Vernon sneak out of church on the Sunday that the gun went missing. He had sensed that Vernon was worried that this woman might remember seeing him leave the church and might be able to connect him with the theft of the rifle.

The police were able to locate Emma Higgins with no difficulty. Even if Dr. Langsner's description had been less specific, they would still have been able to find her. She always sat at the back of the church so that she could see everything — who sat with whom, who was late, who snuck out early. If anyone had noticed Vernon leave, it would have been spinster Higgins. When the police met with Higgins, she was able to tell them not only when Vernon had left, but how long he had been gone from church before sneaking back again.

Constable Olsen was now confident that he had enough to charge Vernon with the quadruple homicide. He met with Vernon, told him that they had found the gun, told him that they could tie him in with the theft of the gun, and told him that they knew his motive for the murders. Vernon initially denied the allegations, but then broke down and confessed. He had indeed hated his mother. Not only had she insulted the girl he loved, but she had forbidden him to see her again. Vernon had been fed up with her interfering in his life, tired of her telling him what he could and could not do. The other murders, he said, had not been planned. He had simply panicked when he realized that they would be able to tie him to the murder of his mother. He expressed neither sorrow nor remorse.

On April 26, 1929, Vernon Booher was hanged at Fort Saskatchewan for the murder of four people. Dr. Langsner died that same year in Fairbanks, Alaska, where he had travelled to do research on telepathy and mind control among the Inuit.

Psychic Archaeology: Dr. Emerson and George McMullen
In early 1960, Ann Emerson, wife of one of Canada's preeminent archaeologists, attended a lecture on clairvoyance. The type of clairvoyance that was described was different than any Ann was familiar with. It looked into the remote past rather than the present or future. Ann became very excited. She had gone to the lecture because she felt the skill

Clairvoyants

might be useful to her husband.

Dr. Norman Emerson was an authority on the ancient peoples of Ontario — the Huron, Ojibwa, Iroquois, and Cree, among others. From scattered fragments of material found at archaeological digs, he pieced together the mode of life of people who lived hundreds and thousands of years ago. The potential for the use of the clairvoyant technique was better than she had dared hope.

The meeting that Ann attended might have been only an evening's entertainment, but instead it was to be the start of a partnership that was to turn the beliefs of archaeologists on their heads. For at that meeting were two important people — Lottie McMullen and her husband, bush guide George McMullen. Ann learned that George McMullen had possessed psychic abilities since childhood. Foretelling the death of a local teenager, he had been accused by the local clergy of "having relations with the Devil." So McMullen had learned to keep silent after that. Later, he had met another psychic, an older man, who valued McMullen's gift and helped him develop it.

Ann was intrigued and told her husband. He scoffed at the idea of psychic abilities, but Ann persisted. When she next met the McMullens, she told George of her husband's ill health. Did he have any suggestions that might help? McMullen had never met Emerson, but was able to describe his medical ailments with such accuracy that Ann felt as if he'd had access to her husband's medical chart. She knew her husband would be impressed with McMullen's ability.

There was nothing in McMullen's education that would suggest medical knowledge. He'd had to drop out of school to find work when still a young boy. Yet he had been able to make recommendations for treatment — recommendations that caused a swift and remarkable recovery in Emerson's health. Emerson reasoned that if McMullen could "read" people he had never met, there was reasonable ground to suggest that he might be able to read archaeological sites and artefacts. He decided to put McMullen to the test.

Emerson handed McMullen a fragment of pottery discovered at the Black Creek archaeological site. He quietly held it in his hands. After several minutes, he told Emerson that the object was a pipe stem and gave him the location and the site from which it had come. McMullen then provided information on the maker of the pipe, the process by which it was made, and details of the community from whence it had come.

Most astoundingly, McMullen was able to draw a picture of the pipe bowl that would have been on the pipe stem. It seemed he received a complete visual image of the original object.

Emerson was impressed, but he was a scientist and wanted more evidence. He took McMullen to the Iroquois Quackenbush village site, north of Peterborough, Ontario. Emerson wanted him to "read" the site. McMullen handled some kernels of corn. He announced that they were not grown there.

Clairvoyants

Emerson was puzzled. It was common knowledge that the Iroquois traditionally grew corn, beans, and squash. So commonly were they grown together that the crops were known as "the Three Sisters." However, McMullen's reading of the artefacts at the site was different. He was adamant: the Iroquois had not grown these crops.

Emerson wondered whether McMullen was really as clairvoyant as he had thought. The evidence from his fellow scientists had shown ample evidence of these crops on the site. Was something interfering with McMullen's ability to "read" the kernels? Emerson decided to do more studies on the kernels that were causing so much conflict within the group of scientists. He transported some kernels to his lab. The microscopic test was conclusive.

The kernels of corn handled by McMullen had not been grown at the Quackenbush Iroquois village. They showed an entirely different construction than the local corn. McMullen had been right — trade with other tribes had brought this corn there.

In 1973, Emerson presented his findings to the Canadian Archaeological Association. His peers were dismayed and more than a little embarrassed that someone as eminent as Emerson would believe in this nonsense called "intuitive archaeology." They considered asking him to resign from the association, but Emerson was the founding vice-president. Perhaps it was his health, they said. In actuality, he had been looking much fitter lately.

The challenge was on; McMullen had to be discredited. At the annual association banquet, fellow archaeologist Jack Miller brought a piece of argillite, or black stone. It appeared to be a very crudely carved Negroid head. Strangely, it had been found on the Queen Charlotte Islands, off the coast of British Columbia. McMullen held the head in his hands. He remained still for many moments and then spoke with certainty, claiming the carver of the head was "a Negro from Port-au-Prince in the Caribbean." McMullen added that the carver had come to Canada as a slave.

Emerson was worried. The reading seemed unlikely. Perhaps McMullen was losing his skills. He kept the carving, thinking that they could try again at a later date. When they did try later, the result was the same, except that McMullen added new details. He now said that the slave had come from the Caribbean, but had been born in West Africa, where he had been captured and sold into slavery. In the Caribbean, he had been sold again and transported to Canada on an English ship. McMullen added that the man had escaped from slavery, and had been taken in by a Native tribe. Finally, McMullen said that the one-time slave had married one of the Native women and had remained with the tribe until his death.

Emerson didn't know what to do. He had gone out on a limb to tell of the innovative work that he and McMullen had done together. Had he made a professional fool of himself? He spoke with his family. His college-aged daughter Linley had a suggestion. Her roommate did Tarot readings. Why not see what her reading showed? Emerson agreed. He felt he had nothing to lose at this point. He handed the head to the young woman.

"What do you see?" asked Emerson.

His daughter's roommate told them that the "head had been carved by a black from Africa who had been brought across the Atlantic as a slave." Emerson was relieved but curious. How had such a carving, with such a history, ended up in the Queen Charlotte Islands? He approached other psychics at every opportunity. More details emerged. The slave had come from a village 50 kilometres inland from the coast of West Africa. Another tribesman, not a white slave ship, had captured the man, but he had eventually been sold to a slave ship.

Emerson went back to the world of academe. With so many corroborating readings, he felt more sure of McMullen's capabilities. He took the carving to the Royal Ontario Museum and asked the opinion of a cultural anthropologist. The answer surprised and gratified him, for the professor said that someone who "was familiar with the art techniques of the Gold Coast of West Africa" had carved it.

Two years later, McMullen was vindicated finally and brilliantly. A team of anthropologists doing blood analysis research on the West Coast Indians detected unmistakable proof of black heritage among the people. McMullen had been right. The carver of the argillite head had not only married into the tribe, he had fathered children.

Bibliography

Aubrey, Claude. *The Magic Fiddler and Other Legends of French Canada*. Toronto, Ontario: Clarke Irwin, 1968.

Blais, J.M. "Edouard Beaupre 1881 – 1904." *Canadian Medical Association Journal*. 96: 1647 -1653.

Burden, George and Grant, Dorothy. *Amazing Medical Stories*. Fredericton, New Brunswick: Goose Lane Editions, 2003.

Cleary, Val. *Ghost Stories of Canada*. Willowdale, Ontario: Hounslow Press, 1985.

Colombo, John Robert. *Mysterious Canada: Strange Sights, Extra-ordinary Events and Peculiar Places*. Toronto, Ontario: Doubleday, 1988.

Dickson, Doris. "Dr. Locke and His Million Dollar Thumbs" in *Maclean's Canada*. Toronto, Ontario: McClelland and Stewart Ltd., 1960.

Fowke, Edith. *Folklore of Canada.* Toronto, Ontario: McClelland and Stewart Ltd., 1976.

Lambert,R.S. *Exploring the Supernatural: The Weird in Canadian Folklore.* Toronto, Ontario: McClelland and Stewart Ltd., 1955.

McDonald, Neil. T. *The Baldoon Mysteries: A Weird Tale of the Early Scotch Settlers of Baldoon.* Wallaceburg, Ontario: News Office, 1910.

Owen, A.R.G. *Psychic Mysteries of Canada.* Toronto, Ontario: Fitzhenry & Whiteside, 1975.

Owen, E.A. *Pioneer Sketches of Long Point Settlement.* Toronto, Ontario: William Briggs, 1898.

Schellenberg, Ruth. *Lake of the Healing Waters.* California: Star Books, 1996.

Sweeney, John M. Winnipeg Free Press. October 13 – 27, 1934.
Tuttle, Charles. *Tuttle's Popular History of the Dominion of Canada.* Moncton, New Brunswick: H.B.Bigney, 1877.

Wilson, Colin. *The Psychic Detectives: Paranormal Crime Detection, Telepathy and Psychic Archaeology.* San Francisco, California: Mercury House, 1985.

Acknowledgments

The author wishes to acknowledge the following sources for their assistance with the manuscript: Dale Swan for his personal stories about his great grand-aunt Anna Swan; Margaret Evans, RCMP historian, for helping me sort out the intricacies of RCMP/Alberta Provincial Police history; Theresa Myroniuk, librarian at the Manville Public Library, for taking the time to read to me from a book in their collection; Christine Jack of the Harriet Irving Library Microfiche Collection at the University of New Brunswick for her assistance in finding elusive articles; Joanne Cole of the Harvey Community Library for her efforts to find me just what I was looking for; and Anne Ouellette for her assistance with translations.

A note of thanks goes to the Government of Canada for their efforts in recording the history of Canada, and making it available to us on the Internet through www.canadiana. org, and to the tourism departments of the provinces for being unfailingly helpful in responding to my requests for information.

A personal thank you goes to Altitude editor Nancy Mackenzie, whose professional and positive suggestions were much appreciated and resulted in a stronger manuscript. Most of all, I want to thank my family for their unswerving encouragement and tolerance as I researched yet another fascinating facet of Canada's past.

Useful web sites:
www.revue-ndc.gc.ca
http://collections.ic.gc.ca/aswan/story/
www.canadiana.org
http://jupiter.uqo.ca/pilfOI/corriv.html
www.virtualsk.com/current_issue/giant_beaupre.html

Photo Credits

Cover: The Willow Bunch Museum; Dale Swan: page 21; Artist: Alfred Laliberté/Musée national des beaux-arts du Quebec/Jean-Guy Kerouac/34.427: page 55; Stanya: page 133; The Willow Bunch Museum: page 33.

About the Author

 Johanna Bertin is a freelance writer who makes her home in Smithfield, New Brunswick. Her feature articles, essays, and book reviews have appeared in publications across Canada.

Johanna came to her love of Canadian history when removing old newspapers that had been used to insulate the walls of her nineteenth-century farmhouse. The past came alive in these news articles. There were fascinating people and events that had never appeared in any textbook that Johanna had read in school. It is these stories that Johanna chose to tell in *Strange Events and More*, the tales of everyday people whose lives tell us much about Canada and the spirit of Canadians.

Johanna is also the author of *Strange Events: Incredible Canadian Monsters, Curses, Ghosts and other Tales*, Altitude Publishing, 2003. She is presently researching her next book — on Sable Island, Nova Scotia. When she is not writing, she works as a medical social worker in Fredericton, New Brunswick.

AMAZING STORIES™

STRANGE EVENTS

Incredible Canadian Monsters, Curses, Ghosts, and Other Tales

MYSTERY/HISTORY
by Johanna Bertin

STRANGE EVENTS

Incredible Canadian Monsters, Curses, Ghosts, and Other Tales

"Nicholson was shocked when a 'dazzling light and shrieking whistle' came out of nowhere and headed right for his train. Paralysed with fear, he... swore that the passengers in the ghost train's lighted cars had looked directly at him."

What are the chances of being hit by lightening three times in one lifetime? And then, being hit again after you are dead and buried? This is just one of the incredible legends in this fascinating collection. From ghosts lurking on board mystery ships to the dark and chilling secrets of Niagara's devil's playground, Canada's history has never been so thrilling.

True stories. Truly Canadian.

ISBN 1-55153-952-7

also available!

AMAZING STORIES™

ONTARIO MURDERS

Mysteries, Scandals, and
Dangerous Criminals

CRIME/MYSTERY
by Susan McNicoll

ONTARIO MURDERS
Mysteries, Scandals, and Dangerous Criminals

"From an early age, lying came easily to her.
Everything she did was a performance, a role
she played to create an illusion."
From the story of Evelyn Dick

Six chilling stories of notorious Ontario murders are recounted in this spine-tingling collection. From the pretty but dangerous Evelyn Dick to the mysterious murder of one of the Fathers of Confederation, Thomas D'Darcy McGee, these stories will keep you on the edge of your seat.

True stories. Truly Canadian.

ISBN 1-55153-951-9

AMAZING STORIES

also available!

AMAZING STORIES™

THE BLACK DONNELLYS

The Outrageous Tale of
Canada's Deadliest Feud

CRIME/BIOGRAPHY
by Nate Hendley

THE BLACK DONNELLYS
The Outrageous Tale of
Canada's Deadliest Feud

*"Johannah trained her sons to fight dirty.
A knee to the groin, a thumb to an eye, all
was fair as long as a Donnelly prevailed.
'Hit first, talk later,' she told her boys."*

The gruesome saga of the Black Donnellys has been heavily mythologized. A thick layer of rumour, legend, and hearsay has built up around the facts of the case. But one thing is clear. No one who reads this book will ever forget the murderous events that occurred near the town of Lucan, Ontario in the 1870s.

True stories. Truly Canadian.

ISBN 1-55153-943-8

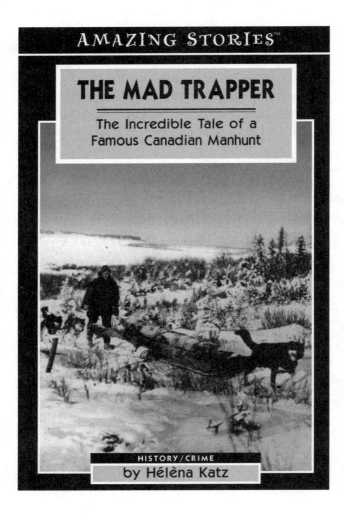

THE MAD TRAPPER

The Incredible Tale of a
Famous Canadian Manhunt

"His lips were curled back in an ugly sneer, and his teeth looked like fangs sticking out through his beard. Johnson hadn't found the peace in death that had eluded him in the last weeks of his life."

This is the incredible story of Canada's largest manhunt. Hundreds of men spent 7 weeks tracking the elusive Albert Johnson for 240 kilometres across the frozen North. He was eventually caught and killed but the identity of Albert Johnson, the Mad Trapper of Rat River, remains a mystery to this day.

True stories. Truly Canadian.

ISBN 1-55153-787-7

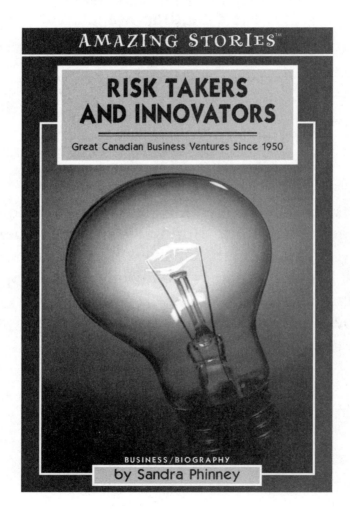

RISK TAKERS AND INNOVATORS
Great Canadian Business Ventures Since 1950

"Surely it can't be that difficult. After all, everything under the sun has to be invented by someone. Why not me?"
Roy Mayer, Inventor

Harnessing their creativity, technology skills, and entrepreneurship, the tenacious individuals featured in these stories have realized their dreams and, in many cases, developed their innovation into a viable business venture. From the first glimmer of an idea to the fruition of the invention, these great Canadian discoveries are an inspiration to aspiring inventors and entrepreneurs everywhere.

True stories. Truly Canadian.

ISBN 1-55153-974-8

OTHER AMAZING STORIES

ISBN	Title	Author
1-55153-943-8	Black Donnellys	Nate Hendley
1-55153-947-0	Canada's Rumrunners	Art Montague
1-55153-966-7	Canadian Spies	Tom Douglas
1-55153-795-8	D-Day	Tom Douglas
1-55153-982-9	Dinosaur Hunters	Lisa Murphy-Lamb
1-55153-970-5	Early Voyageurs	Marie Savage
1-55153-968-3	Edwin Alonzo Boyd	Nate Hendley
1-55153-996-9	Emily Carr	Cat Klerks
1-55153-973-X	Great Canadian Love Stories	Cheryl MacDonald
1-55153-946-2	Great Dog Stories	Roxanne Snopek
1-55153-942-X	The Halifax Explosion	Joyce Glasner
1-55153-958-6	Hudson's Bay Company Adventures	Elle Andra-Warner
1-55153-969-1	Klondike Joe Boyle	Stan Sauerwein
1-55153-980-2	Legendary Show Jumpers	Debbie G-Arsenault
1-55153-979-9	Ma Murray	Stan Sauerwein
1-55153-964-0	Marilyn Bell	Patrick Tivy
1-55153-953-5	Moe Norman	Stan Sauerwein
1-55153-962-4	Niagara Daredevils	Cheryl MacDonald
1-55153-945-4	Pierre Elliott Trudeau	Stan Sauerwein
1-55153-981-0	Rattenbury	Stan Sauerwein
1-55153-991-8	Rebel Women	Linda Kupecek
1-55153-956-X	Robert Service	Elle Andra-Warner
1-55153-952-7	Strange Events	Johanna Bertin
1-55153-954-3	Snowmobile Adventures	Linda Aksomitis
1-55153-950-0	Tom Thomson	Jim Poling Sr.
1-55153-976-4	Trailblazing Sports Heroes	Joan Dixon
1-55153-977-2	Unsung Heroes of the RCAF	Cynthia J. Faryon
1-55153-959-4	A War Bride's Story	Cynthia Faryon
1-55153-948-9	The War of 1812 Against the States	Jennifer Crump

These titles are available wherever you buy books. If you have trouble finding the book you want, call the Altitude order desk at 1-800-957-6888, e-mail your request to: orderdesk@altitudepublishing.com or visit our Web site at www.amazingstories.ca

New AMAZING STORIES titles are published every month.